THE ASTROLOGICAL
BODY TYPES

FACE, FORM, AND EXPRESSION

*Written and Illustrated
by
Judith A. Hill*

Revised and Expanded Edition

STELLIUM
PRESS

THE ASTROLOGICAL BODY TYPES:
Face, Form and Expression by Judith A. Hill

Published by Stellium Press, Portland, OR

ISBN 0-945685-21-1
ISBN

Library of Congress Catalog Number 97-070867

Printed in the United States of America

Third Edition, Revised

*For
Jennie,
who loved humanity*

ACKNOWLEDGMENTS

Editors:

First Edition: Susan Payton & Donna Jaeger

Second Edition: Michael Theroux & Brian Butler

Third Edition: Dawn King (edit & re-design)
Cover by Seth T. Miller

Special thanks to:

R. M. Hill

Katherine Ace

Mark Ace

Joan Margalith

Robert Briggs

Janis Mennona

Madaline Allen

Trish Turchiarolo

Matthew Giannetti

And for inspiration: Gina O'Feral

TABLE OF CONTENTS

LIST OF TABLES & FIGURES

PREFACE

The Planetary, Elemental and Zodiacal Sign Types are very ancient. One reads of physical characteristics attributed to various planetary positions within the birth chart in Ptolemy's "The Form and Temperament of the Body,"[1] 140 c.e. We also know that Ptolemy copied much of his material from considerably older sources at the later-to-be-burned Library of Alexandria. There is no doubt that the astrologer-priests of antiquity corresponded the planets with human physical types. For instance, the ancient Syrians sacrificed red-headed men to the red planet-god Mars!

Physical characteristics were also associated with the twelve zodiac signs at an early date. Chiefly, these simple descriptions relate diseases, fertility, unusual births, twins and an impressive host of disabilities to the Sun, Moon and various planetary combinations being posited in specific zodiac signs at birth.

By the Middle Ages, we find exhaustive physical narratives on the twelve signs, inclusive of detail for all planets through each sign of the zodiac! A sophisticated Medical Astrology also existed by this time, with planetary and zodiacal assignments to each bodily part and organ, plus a comprehensive knowledge of the physical/medical affects of the four elements [see Appendices].

What actually are the zodiac sign "types" as we know them in Western astrology? To answer this, the reader must first understand that the Western, or "tropical" zodiac signs are *seasons*, and not *constellations*, as one might suppose. These seasons are thirty days each in duration. The starting point of the seasonal wheel is always the exact moment of the Spring Equinox. This event, representing an exact Earth/Sun light and space relationship, always establishes

---

[1] A chapter of his *Tretrabiblios*

the first day of the first sign, or season, Aries. Because the human being is the only mammal capable of giving birth all year round, it is possible that these twelve seasonal types may actually reflect twelve conception types, and consequentially their *in utero* preparation for the seasonal conditions of their upcoming birth, nine months later.[2]

Astrologically speaking, zodiac signs are hybrids of both a seasonal and a planetary type. All signs are traditionally classified according to "element," "mode," and also ruling planet, and each of these has physical characteristics that blend together in creating your astrological sign type. You will find the complete details on these astrological "building blocks" included in this book.

For example, a "Taurus" is a person born between thirty and sixty days after the Spring Equinox. This season is of the element "Earth," the mode is "Fixed," and the ruling planet is Venus, with a secondary influence of the Moon. These astrological energies may work independently, or in combination, to reflect themselves in the Taurus individual. Of course, as you will soon discover, your Moon sign, Ascendant, and particularly the strongest planets in your birth chart may also describe your physical appearance.

A lifetime of research and about nine thousand personal consultations have established the background material for this book. Additionally, I've read everything I could find on the subject of *astrophysiognomy* by previous authors, ancient and modern. My forays into this fascinating field have led me to conclude that independently cited similar observations are the rule, rather than the exception. Unfortunately however, it would not be possible to include, much less to know of all extant opinions on the subject. Those readers seeking scientific validation for this work will find the statistical and research material in Appendix 3 to be of great interest.

---

[2] This interesting hypothesis is Edmund Van Deussen's, from his book *Astro-Genetics*.

My intent has been to unite in one volume comprehensive descriptions of the physical appearance and "mood" of each traditional planetary, zodiacal sign, elemental and modal type, thus providing the student with a useful compendium. Herein the reader may find, to his/her interest and enjoyment, the most frequently cited observations (my own and others) of the traditional astrological body types.

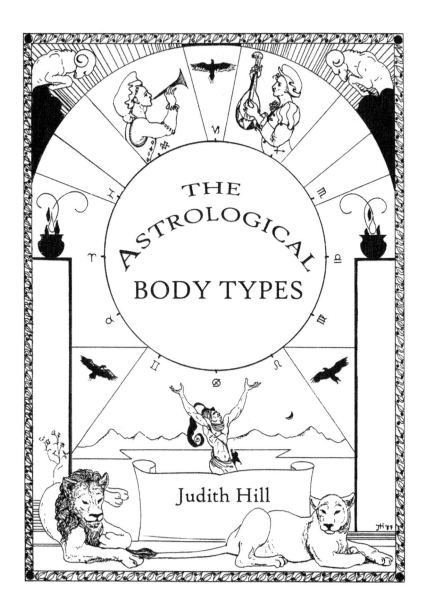

THE
ASTROLOGICAL
BODY TYPES

Judith Hill

INTRODUCTION TO ASTROPHYSIOGNOMY

What does it take to make a rose?
It takes the world's eternal wars,
The Sun and Moon and all the stars,
It takes the might of heaven and hell,
And everlasting love as well.

– Alfred Noyes

Astrophysiognomy is the branch of Astrology studying correlations between the birth chart and physical appearance. The underlying theory is simple: We look like what we think and feel. We can state this another way by saying that the planetary birth chart is a sort of composite map of our conscious and unconscious minds. The qualities of our minds express themselves in many ways and some of these ways are physical. The way we look is to a large extent mirrored by the planetary positions at our birth. The voice, manner, gesture and choice of attire are some examples of the physical expression of mental and emotional states.

Our genetic heritage is, of course, a significant player in physical appearance. The infant body we first inhabit presents us with a definite genetic package, that influences us—as well as being influenced by us, as we mold our bodies and faces with persistent thought and feeling. Our body's genetic code is a precise set of instructions for creating physical forms. A gene pool is a distinct set of thoughts with a distinct intention. A gene is itself a thought!

Genetics is used as a favorite argument against Astrophysiognomy. But gene pools are not exempt from the theories of Astrophysiognomy. At conception a soul attracts from its genetic pool—the pool of encoded thoughts handed down from generation to generation—the physical qualities and attributes that best reflect its nature. For various reasons souls are attracted to the entire thought atmosphere of the parents, inclusive of the parental genetic material.

When you inherit your father's nose, you also inherit the thoughts and feelings that express themselves as his nose. Throughout the many stages of life, the embodied soul continues to work with its given genetic material, subtly altering it's outward expression. Each entity possesses individuality and free choice and must choose or create its own thoughts, feelings, and actions. As we build our minds, so we build our faces. It has been said that by the time we are forty, we have the faces we deserve!

The countenance is the portrait of the mind,
the eyes its informers.
– Cicero

The endless variation of birth charts is mirrored by the un-limited variety of human faces and bodies. An awareness of archetypal themes woven amidst this diversity is useful for understanding people, and essential for astrologers. Skill in this field grows with experience.

Previous works on Astrophysiognomy mainly discuss the "effects" of planets and signs upon the outward appearance of the face, bodily form, and manner. Rarely are underlying causes discussed, and we are left with a documentation of effects, without an explanation of cause.

So it is imperative to begin our exploration of Astrophysi-ognomy with a clear statement: ***Planets and signs describe but do not cause physical appearance.*** John is not red-headed because the red planet Mars was prominent at birth. Rather, his red hair is described or mirrored in his birth chart by a prominent Mars. A wide array of mental and emotional traits would also be signaled by a strong Mars in John's birth chart. Should the gene for red hair be unavailable in John's gene pool, a "martial" temperament could express itself facially and bodily in a great number of other ways. It is also quite likely that one of John's parents, and some of his siblings might also have been born when Mars was in prominence.

An important Astrophysiognomical rule is that the gene pool takes the path of least resistance relative to the horoscope. Should our ancestors be mostly blonde, it will not be possible to have black hair, no matter what the chart suggests. The astrological indications of dark hair may produce merely darker hair—or express themselves in another way entirely. Similarly, the fairest children in a family will tend to have the "fairest" birth charts.

Naturally, what is considered fair or dark differs dramatically between India and Norway. The Astrophysiognomy student is loudly cautioned to first establish what is possible for the observed genetic type. One may, for instance, find a very "tall" birth chart having a surprising owner of merely five feet eight inches tall. Upon inquiring, you may discover this man to be a real giant in his village where men rarely achieve five feet four! Relativity-to-the-genetic-type is very important because most Astrophysiognomical observations are of persons of Caucasian descent. Unfortunately, no Western Astrophysiognomy text presents an adequate analysis for racial groups other than the Caucasian, and much research is needed.

It is quite true that some (but by no means all) modern scientists vehemently reject the old astrological axiom, "As above, so below," which is the philosophical basis of Astrophysiognomy. But it is equally true that the great mystics and magi of all ages would see this rejection of Universal Oneness as illogical!

TABLE 1
PRINCIPLES OF ASTROPHYSIOGNOMY

- Planets and Signs *reflect* but do not *cause* physical appearance.

- Genes are inherited instructions—or thoughts—that program physical form. Established physical structure is further molded by dominant thoughts and feelings.

- Thoughts and feelings—structure and expression—can be categorized or classed by planetary type and sign type.

- The features, forms and coloration suggested by the planetary birth chart respond along a "path of least resistance" to the material available within an individual's gene-pool.

- A planet will only express physically what is within the possible genetic range. Do not expect extraordinary physical traits suggested by the birth chart to occur when such traits are a genetic impossibility for that individual.

- Without a great familiarity of facial parameters and characteristics of any given racial group, you are in absolutely no position to perform a facial analysis of an individual of that group (*see "About Race," next page*).

- Our faces, voices and bodies are influenced by how we think and feel. Thoughts and feelings affect bodily appearance in different ways.

- Each planetary and sign class of thoughts and feelings possesses both a positive and a negative potential and can be used in a spiritually constructive or destructive manner, dependent on the will of the thinker. Each planetary and sign class of thoughts and feelings possesses a range of expression from the most crude to the most refined.

- The facial expression, habitual body posture plus the vibrational atmosphere of an individual must always be given great weight in the total analysis (*see "Facial Expression – How the Features are Used" page 7*).

- There will be exceptions to every rule. Faces show a great deal about character most of the time, but not all of the time.

ABOUT RACE
THE POTENTIAL MISUSE OF ASTROPHYSIOGNOMY

A FORMAL STATEMENT

The purpose of this book is to provide the reader with a useful catalogue of astrological types—their character and appearance. The astrological body types exist for all races. However, these astro-physical types are in no way identical to, nor should they be confused with racial types.

Attempts to apply any of the astrological body types in support of racial or gender-based doctrines would constitute a gross misinterpretation of this material.

It is imperative to remember that the information in this book was developed from the observation of Caucasian, Semitic and East Indian populations. Without an intimate familiarity with the extremes and distinctive features found within a given race, we are in absolutely no position to perform facial analysis for members of that race.

It is even possible that African, Asian and Caucasian faces have their own rules. For example, Chinese face-reading manuals provide extensive descriptions of Asian eye types and their meanings. Caucasian eyes, possessing no true epicanthus (the distinctive eye fold of the Asian eye) cannot be properly understood according to the Chinese system.

5

It is also true that all races could use this material once a range of normal form types is established for their given genetic group. For example, when we say "broad forms," we mean broader than average according to the norms of the race. Most African people may appear to have broad forms to an observing European.

Similarly, to an African, most Europeans would appear to have narrow or thin forms. Yet, we can observe great variance of form type within this generally narrow range. All races have normal, broad, and full forms according to their own overall norms. It takes time and familiarity to accurately evaluate the range of forms for persons of racial heritage other than one's own. The advice here is to stick to what you know.

BUILDING BLOCKS
OF ASTROPHYSIOGNOMY
FACIAL EXPRESSION
HOW THE FEATURES ARE USED

The analysis of expression and "vibrational atmosphere" is perhaps the most important and most neglected aspect of the face reader's art. The habitual posture of an eye or mouth tells as much, if not more, about character than the shape. One noteworthy example is the face of Elisabeth Kubler-Ross, a woman whose broad and generous expression belies her rather thin, sharp features. Such examples are not uncommon.

The psychic or "vibrational atmosphere" is a thing that must be intuitively sensed and rarely exerts itself through photographs in a reliable way. Obviously, person-to-person character analysis is vastly superior to the study of portraits or photos. Texts that are exclusively devoted to an analysis of facial forms may prove misleading. If we wish to be accurate, expression and atmosphere must be taken into account. Therefore, pay special attention to the sections on "Manner" preceding each planetary and sign type description.

BROAD AND FULL FORMS

[See: Jupiter, Venus, Moon, Sun, Neptune, Taurus, Pisces, Cancer, Sagittarius]

Broad, inclusive thoughts and feelings

More expansive than restrictive

More generous than critical

More emotional than logical

More intuitive than rational

SHARP, POINTED AND NARROW FORMS

[See: Mercury, Mars, Saturn, Pluto; also Aries, Scorpio, Virgo, Capricorn, Gemini]

Narrow, defined thoughts and feelings

Sharp-minded

More critical and logical than emotional or intuitive

Sharp, analytical, intellectual, scrutinizing

SOFT, PLIABLE, ELASTIC FORMS

[See: Mercury, Neptune, Gemini, Pisces, Libra]

Affectionate, easy-going, amiable, romantic

Compassionate

More flexible than fixed

More yielding than controlling

Weak-willed, sweet-natured, non-ambitious and indirect

Sometimes evasive, indecisive, or deceptive

QUICK, MOBILE FORMS

[See: Mercury, Uranus, Gemini, Aquarius]

Expressive, humorous, lively, quick-thinking, clever

Shallow, manually dexterous, coordinated

Able with language

SLOW, HEAVY OR IMMOBILE FORMS

[See: Taurus, Capricorn Type 2, Scorpio, Earth]

Unflappable, fixed, obstinate, unfeeling or dull

Enduring

BULGING FORMS

[See: Moon, Jupiter, Neptune, Pisces, Taurus, Cancer, Gemini, Sagittarius]

Extroverted, talkative

Poor sense of social boundaries and order

Excessive and expressive, witty

Sometimes hyperactive, intrusive

ANGULAR, SQUARE FORMS

[See: Fire signs, Saturn, Pluto, Mars, Aries, Taurus, Leo, Scorpio, Capricorn]

Energetic, physical, athletic, hard-working, enduring

Combative, ambitious, stubborn, proud and impatient

SMOOTH ROUND FORMS

[See: Water signs, Moon, Venus, Jupiter, Taurus, Cancer, Pisces]

Emotional, nurturing, receptive, sociable, yielding

Musical, Poetic

Joyful, fun-loving, playful, humorous

Trivial, illogical, near-sighted and childlike

OVAL, GRACEFUL, SYMMETRICAL FORMS

[See: Venus, Neptune, Libra, Pisces, Air]

Poised and amiable nature

Gentle, artistic, social

More observant than initiating

Diplomatic, tasteful, refined and cultured

Sometimes vain, irresolute and weak-willed

TIGHT, HIDDEN, PROTECTED FORMS

[See: Saturn, Pluto, Lunar Type 1, Cancer, Capricorn, Scorpio, Virgo]

Introverted, cautious, defensive, contemplative

Critical, self-controlled, controlling, stingy

FLARING FORMS (NOSTRILS OR LIPS)

[See: Fire signs, Sun, Mars, Leo, Aries]

Prideful, arrogant, disdainful, irreverent

Powerful, vain, influential, willful, hot-tempered, sardonic

TIGHT, HIDDEN, PROTECTED FORMS

[See: Saturn, Pluto, Lunar Type 1, Cancer, Capricorn, Scorpio, Virgo]

Introverted, cautious, defensive, contemplative

Critical, self-controlled, controlling, stingy

FLARING FORMS (NOSTRILS OR LIPS)

[See: Fire signs, Sun, Mars, Leo, Aries]

Prideful, arrogant, disdainful, irreverent

Powerful, vain, influential, willful, hot-tempered, sardonic

THE FACE IN GENERAL
NON-ASTROLOGICAL OBSERVATIONS

There is very little research describing how the psyche is expressed by one facial feature over another. The following list, drawn from several sources as well as the author's extensive observations, is offered as suggestions for further exploration.

THE UPPER FACE

Forehead, cheekbones, eyes and nose.
The region of thought, intellect, imagination and reason.
The higher "human" faculties and spiritual qualities.

THE FOREHEAD

1. Top of head: spiritual, inspirational and venerational faculties; the imagination; creative thought.

2. Upper forehead: the seat of analytical and reasoning faculties.

3. Middle forehead: memory faculties; sense of time and place.

4. Lower forehead, brows: the "engineer" faculties; ability to observe and categorize objects and facts; practical, observation skills.

THE EYES

"The window of the soul." The entity who inhabits the physical body is best known through the eyes. The eternal qualities that identify the individuality from life to life are found in the eyes. These qualities may be distinct from the personality, qualities of the body, and genetic influences.

THE NOSE
The nature and power of the intellect and mental force. Projection of one's ideas and actions into the outer world. The degree of decisiveness and combativeness. The will of the mind and the ability to govern the instincts. The execution of activity. Investigative, analytical and scrutinizing faculties. Curiosity. Individuality.

THE CHEEKBONES
The breadth and height of the cheek appears to indicate managerial ability, practical and financial executive qualities and authority. They also relate to sex appeal and power over others.

THE LOWER FACE
The lips, mouth, chin and jaw line.
The region of the instinctual drives, animal will, physical force, endurance, appetite, stamina, resistance.

THE MOUTH
The sensual and social impulses. Moral nature, emotional and sexual nature and type of expression, ability to love, affection, acceptance level, receptivity.

THE UPPER LIP
The lip of love and affection. Sense of beauty, melody, sweetness, romance, desires and emotional needs. Refinement and sensitivity level, eloquence.

THE LOWER LIP
Sexual desire and aggressiveness.
Physical self-control (or lack of).

THE CHIN

Physical strength and energy.
Stubborn resistance, determination.

THE JAW

Physical endurance, stability, follow-through. The level of independent action. Aggressiveness and courage. Toughness and backbone. The need for leg-activity. Ability to carry the ideas (forehead) and actions (nose) into completion.

LEFT FACE/RIGHT FACE

Most individuals show great variance between their left and right facial hemispheres. The degree of difference may depend in part on the complexity of their personality. People with great conflicts within themselves may reflect these conflicts in the creation of two very different sides of their faces.

Through photo-trickery, two left halves and two right sides of one face can be made to form two new faces that often appear completely different from each other and the face of origin. The left face expresses a more latent, less dominant or subconscious side of the personality, while the right side is thought to describe the more conscious and outgoing side. Similarly, the left side may indicate our more yielding, emotional or creative parts, while the right reveals the more logical and aggressive aspects of ourselves. Whether or not all of the above reverses itself in left-handed individuals has yet to be researched.

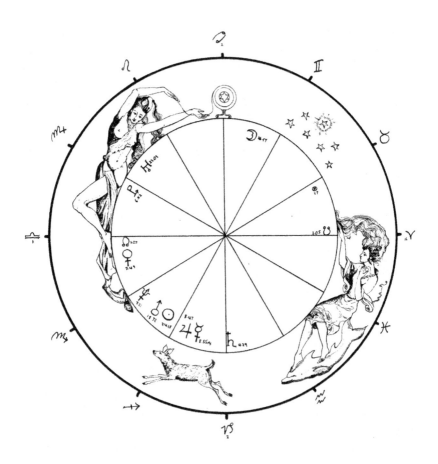

14

THE ELEMENTS AND THE MODES

THE ELEMENTS

Each of the twelve zodiacal signs belongs to one of the four elements: *Fire, Earth, Air,* or *Water.* The fiery, airy, watery, and earthy signs form our first and simplest description of zodiacal types. Frequently, we notice the dominant element of a friend before their more particular sign type.

In the most arcane sense, the elements refer to four levels of increasing concretization of matter: photon, particle, atom, and molecule. One can think of this as the journey of light (the photon) from complete freedom into gradually denser and more predictable forms, until it finds itself "trapped" in the dense material form of the molecule. These four stages of involution are reflected in the human being as spiritual, intellectual, emotional, and physical levels.

The elements can also be described as four types of consciousness. *Fire* symbolizes pure being, the sense of "I," and the life force. It is direct experience. *Air* represents the intellect. This is the world of thought, language and abstraction. Its mode of consciousness is detached observation. Our feeling function is *Water.* Emotions and instincts arise from this level. *Water* is responsive and subjective experience. *Earth* is sensation and the survival instinct. This is the densest of the four levels and corresponds to body consciousness, materiality, and the physical plane.

Individuals can possess an abundance or absence of one or more of these elements, manifesting on all the levels: physical, emotional, psychological and spiritual. Ancient physicians and modern Ayurvedic doctors analyze the balances of the elements in the physical body, noting either abundances or absences.

A person possessing a preponderance of one element is assumed to operate largely within the corresponding level of consciousness symbolized by that element.

Of course, all of the elements have actual physical correspondences. Fire is fire, air is air, water is really water and earth is the earth in your garden. Water types may suffer from water retention. They love to be near lakes or oceans, and they weep easily. Persons with too much Fire are hot and dry. Emotionally, they may be very explosive. Earthy types have heavy bones and strong bodies. They love gardening, baking and building. Those born with an excess of Air in their charts will insist on open windows and enjoy heights and views. These folks are talkative and thin, lacking much of the calm gravity of Earth.

THE FOUR ELEMENTS

BODY SHAPES:

EARTH	WATER	AIR	FIRE
□	○		▽

WATER
THE FEELING TYPE

The Water type results from an excess or preponderance of the Water signs (Pisces, Cancer, Scorpio) and is augmented by a strong Jupiter, Moon, Neptune, Venus or the sign Taurus. *Note:* Water signs are hirsute (productive of abundant body hair).

> *Body Type:* endomorphic (soft and round)
>
> *Traditional Temperament:* phlegmatic
>
> *Body Shape:* round or pear-shaped
>
> *Metabolism:* slow; cool-bodied
>
> *Jungian Type:* feeling

CHARACTER TRAITS:

Sociable, affectionate, domestic, nurturing, protective, peaceful, indulgent, sensual, food-loving, emotional, slow, sensitive, lazy, passive, receptive, subjective, kind.

CAREERS:

Mother, nurse, day-care worker, politician, social service worker, healing professional, cook, midwife, psychic, musician, novelist, poet, caretaker, shopkeeper, innkeeper, vintner, tavern keeper, small business owner, real estate broker.

WATER

EARTH

THE SENSATE TYPE

The Earth type results from an excess or preponderance of Earth signs (Taurus, Virgo and Capricorn) and/or Fixed signs (Taurus, Leo, Scorpio, Aquarius).

Body Type: mesomorphic (square, massive, heavy, dense)

Traditional Temperament: melancholic (this designation appears to better serve the Saturnian Type)

Body Shape: square or rectangular

Metabolism: slow; warm-bodied

Jungian Type: sensation

CHARACTER TRAITS

Steadfast, earnest, dependable, productive, possessive, realistic, materialistic, patient, strong, enduring tough, insensitive, crude withdrawn, conservative, constructive, down to earth, practical, routine.

CAREERS:

Builder, farmer, bricklayer, truck driver, gardener, heavyweight boxer, businessman, football player, police officer, mover, architect, stonemason, laborer or operator of heavy equipment, craftsperson, buyer.

EARTH

FIRE
THE EXPERIENTIAL TYPE

The Fire type results from an excess or preponderance of the Fire signs (Aries, Leo and Sagittarius) and is augmented by a strong Sun or Mars in the planetary birth-map. *Note:* Fire signs tend to baldness in males.

> *Body Type:* lean and muscular
> *Traditional Temperament:* choleric
> *Body Shape:* triangular, with base at top
> *Jungian Type:* Intuitive

CHARACTER TRAITS:

Out-going, confident, dramatic, experiential, independent, impatient, initiating, energetic, hasty, explosive, arrogant, positive, impulsive. *Fire signs are warm, positive and playful!*

CAREERS:

Performers, band-leaders, showmen, athletes, managers, directors, adventurers, publicity and promotion specialists, entertainment and recreation workers, entrepreneurs, gamblers, explorers, firefighters, pilots, race-car drivers, stunt men, advertising, soldiers.

FIRE

AIR
THE THINKING TYPE

The Air type results from an excess or preponderance of Air signs (Gemini, Libra and Aquarius) and/or an excess or preponderance of Mutable signs (Gemini, Sagittarius—in particular—and Virgo, Pisces). The Air Type is augmented by the planets Mercury, Uranus and Saturn. *Note:* Air signs tend to baldness in males.

> *Body Type:* ectomorphic (long, slender, bony, nervous)
>
> *Traditional Temperament:* sanguine
>
> *Body Shape:* long and linear
>
> *Metabolism:* fast; cool-bodied
>
> *Jungian Type:* thinking

CHARACTER TRAITS:

Nervous, mental, idealistic, inquisitive, talkative, freedom-loving, intellectual, delicate, sensitive, detached, clever, versatile, intelligent, impulsive, energetic, friendly, humane, witty, flighty, eccentric, inventive, uncommitted, hopeful, experimental, ingenious.

Note: The planet Saturn is also associated with ectomorphic body types. However, Saturn produces a slow-moving melancholic temperament more akin to Earth signs. Also, Saturnian body types are bony and stiff quite unlike either the fluid, fast-moving and graceful Air types, or the thick and heavy Earth types.

AIR

CAREERS:

Journalists, columnists, lecturers, writers, messengers, inventors, computer specialists, linguists, electricians, radio announcers, scholars, impressionists, cartoonists, postperson, aviators, traveling salespersons, TV show hosts, interviewers, typists, jugglers, puppeteers, thinkers and idea people, reporters, communicators, rock musicians, instrumentalists, scientists, astrologers.

THE MODES

The four elements previously described represent four distinct planes of matter, vibrating at different rates with four corresponding states of consciousness. Matter moves. The three modes describe the rate of matter in motion. These three rates of motion are known as the *Cardinal, Fixed* and *Mutable* modes.

Each of the four elements expresses itself through three rates of motion. For instance, Fire igniting is *Cardinal*. Fire concentrated in an oven is *Fixed*; dispersed wild-fire is *Mutable*.

It is important to stress that the modal types are apparent as physiognomical indicators only in the case of exceptional predominance, with two or more signs of one modal group highly tenanted in the birth chart. In most cases the modes are quite subordinate to planetary, element and sign types.

CARDINAL TYPE
SELF-INITIATIVE

Combined effect of Aries, Cancer, Libra, Capricorn

The Cardinal Mode depicts vigorous, explosive activity and symbolizes the element first bursting into existence. Cardinal signs always occur at the start of each season on the dates of the equinoxes and solstices. The action of this mode is impulsive and hot. The sign most resembling this modality as a whole is the first cardinal sign, Aries.

PHYSICAL CHARACTERISTICS
See "Fire" type and "Aries" type for physical examples.

CHARACTER TRAITS:

Positive: Highly individualistic, self-starting, excitable, independent, leading enterprising, active

Negative: Erratic, explosive, impulsive, arrogant

FIXED TYPE
STRENGTH/ENDURANCE

Combined effect of Taurus, Leo, Scorpio, Aquarius

The Fixed modality describes the fixing of matter into solid, concretized forms. The four Fixed signs are located at the mid-point of each season and represent the concentration of their particular element. The action of the Fixed modality is enduring and inert. When in abundance, this mode produces a quality and physical type similar to the first Fixed sign, Taurus.

PHYSICAL CHARACTERISTICS

Square, strong, dense, heavy muscles and bones, condensed looking, the classic mesomorph.

See "Earth" type and "Taurus" type for physical examples.

CHARACTER TRAITS:

Positive: Strong, determined, enduring reliable, intense, powerful, concentrated

Negative: Willful, obstinate, jealous, habitual, dull, slow, inflexible, stubborn

MUTABLE TYPE
FLEXIBILITY

Combined effect of Gemini, Virgo, Sagittarius, Pisces

Mutable signs symbolize the transition of one season into another. These four signs always occur at the end of a season when its force is dispersing with a modulating and changing expression. An element in transition (such as water into steam) is in its mutable state. In predominance, the Mutable *type* most resembles the first Mutable *sign*, Gemini.

PHYSICAL CHARACTERISTICS

The Mutable type produces more variety of physical expression than the other modal types. A pronounced Mutable emphasis can physically manifest itself as any one of the four Mutable signs— Gemini, Type 1 Virgo, Type 1 Sagittarius, Type 1 or 2 Pisces. The most typical expression would be the first Air sign, Gemini, or Type 2 Pisces: flexible, graceful, refined, slender, sometimes delicate.

CHARACTER TRAITS:

Positive: Flexible, open-minded, versatile, synthesizing, curious

Negative: Scattered, restless, undirected, weak-willed, irresolute

INTRODUCTION TO THE
PLANETARY AND SIGN TYPES

The following are descriptions of pure planetary and sign types based on personal observation and analysis and the opinions of countless astrologers throughout history. Remember, relatively few people exemplify pure types. Most folks are happy or unhappy combinations of two or more types. For instance, a person may possess a typically Sagittarian build but have a perfect Scorpio face.

Every planetary position in your birth chart indicates something about your mind and therefore your physical appearance. A planet describes certain thoughts and emotions and it is these that really mold and influence our features. Certain planetary positions appear to describe our physical appearance more than others do (*See Table 2*).

The distinctive expression symbolized by each of the twelve zodiac signs is reflected in the physical body, as well as in the emotional, mental and spiritual bodies. The physical descriptions for the signs may be apparent in an individual who has even one significator of physical appearance (*See Table 2, pages 33 – 34*) posited in that sign at birth. Remember many signs are capable of several physical expressions. Be sure to memorize the general sign types and keep in mind the nuances of appearance resulting from the 36 Decanates (*See Table 4, Appendix 2, page171*).

HOW TO BEGIN

When analyzing a chart for physical appearance, use the suggestions in the *Table of Significators of Physical Appearance in the Birth Chart (Table 2)*. To begin, start by obtaining ten accurate birth charts (correct time, date and place of birth) of people you are very familiar with. On a sheet of notebook paper list the first six "Significators of Physical Appearance" and their correlations with your subject's chart.

You may find that your subject is a pure type of his/her Sun, Moon or Ascendant sign—or you may discover your subject's appearance to be a combination of two or more of the first six indicators. Astrologers should allow 25 – 75% weight in assessing physical appearance to categories 1, 2, 3 and 4. (*Important:* There exists no reliable method for determining exactly which of significators 1 through 4 will predominately reflect in the physical appearance.)

Now check significators 5 through 12. Check to see if any of these remaining indicators reflect upon the subject's face, body or manner. Having now established your astro-physical profile, you can tentatively assign the character traits and vocational aptitudes of the dominant planetary, elemental and sign types. Also, once you have established your own or a friend's planetary and sign types you are clued in to the dominant thoughts and emotions as listed under each planet and sign heading.

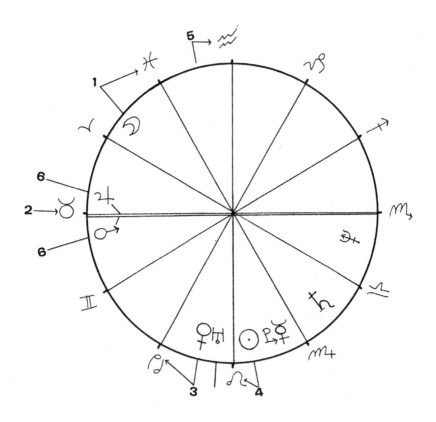

RANDOM CHART (ANONYMOUS)

This figure illustrates six important significators of physical appearance in a birth chart. Refer by number to TABLE 2, (next two pages). An individual's physical appearance will typically be described by at least two of these six factors.

TABLE 2

SIGNIFICATORS OF PHYSICAL APPEARANCE IN THE BIRTH CHART

1. The Moon's sign (especially in females).

2. The Ascending sign (the Ascendant or rising sign)

3. The sign tenanted by the planetary "ruler" of the Ascending sign.

4. The Sun sign. Beware of sign cusps. People born within one or even two days of sign cusps or borders may resemble their neighboring sign. This is most frequent for people born at the tail-end of one sign. This same rule can hold for cusping Ascendants.

5. The opposite sign to the Sun sign. This can be more obvious than the Sun sign for persons born close to sunset or midnight.

6. The planets nearest the Ascending degree (either side of the Ascendant). Planets conjunct the Ascendant take precedence over the sign on the Ascendant; e.g., should Jupiter be rising in Capricorn, the physical appearance will, in most cases, be more Jupiterian than Capricornian.

7. Any planet closely conjunct the planetary ruler of the Ascendant, Sun or Moon.

8. Any sign possessing two or more personal planets, i.e., Mercury, Venus, Mars.

9. The sign position of the decanate ruler of the Ascending sign—often surprisingly prominent!

continues next page

Table 2 continued

10. Any sign possessing a stellium of five or more planets.

11. Stationary planets: This is a planet that has no apparent motion at the time of birth. It is very powerful and may dominate the physical appearance. Consider any planetary stations occurring within one day from birth for Mercury, Venus and Mars and one to three days for slow planets. You will need an Ephemeris to determine the exact speed of specific planets on your date of birth.

12. Dominant Element: Fire, Earth, Air, Water. Look for at least two important indicators such as Sun, Moon, Ascendant, or ruler of Ascendant posited in one element.

13. Dominant Mode. Rare. Must be an overt dominance.

PROFILES OF PLANETARY TYPES

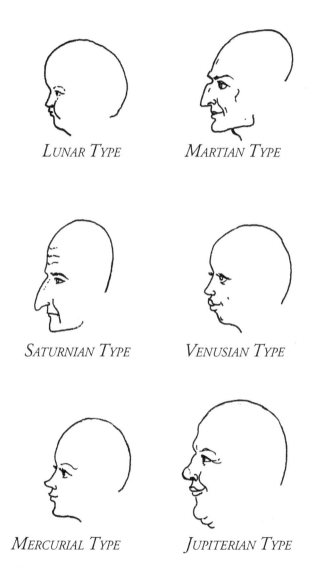

LUNAR TYPE MARTIAN TYPE

SATURNIAN TYPE VENUSIAN TYPE

MERCURIAL TYPE JUPITERIAN TYPE

TABLE 3

CONDITIONS FOR PLANETARY STRENGTH

A "strong" planet in the birth map is a planet that meets one or more of the following conditions. A planet meeting two or more of these conditions becomes *very strong*. An individual may demonstrate the mental emotional and therefore physical traits associated with the strongest planets in their birth map. Weak or neutral planets are those meeting none of the conditions below, in the birth map.

CONDITIONS OF PLANETARY STRENGTH

1. A planet in the sign of either its rulership or exaltation (*See page 40*).

2. A planet within 30° of the Ascendant degree.

3. A planet closely conjunct the Ascendant, Nadir, or Midheaven. All planets are strong conjoined with the Ascendant. Venus, Moon and Jupiter are equally happy near the Nadir. Mars, Saturn and the Sun are best at the Midheaven. Planets are not necessarily strong (physically) near the Descendant degree and may in fact indicate the traits you most need, or the physical and temperamental traits of your partners.

4. A planet closely conjunct the Sun (especially in males) or the Moon (especially in females).

5. A Planet ruling the sign of the birth Sun, Moon or Ascendant.

6. A Planet
    in its *degree of exaltation*:
    Sun . . . . . . *19° Aries*
    Moon . . . *3° Taurus*
    Venus . . . . *27° Pisces*
    Mercury . . *15° Virgo*
    Saturn . . . *21° Libra*
    Mars *28° Capricorn*
    Jupiter . . *15° Cancer*

7. A stationary planet
    (*See number 11 Table 2, page 34*).

8. Singleton planets dominating a hemisphere.
    This is strongest if occurring on the East side
    (left-hand side) of the birth map.

9. Planets within 30° of the Midheaven.

INTERPRETING WEAK OR NEUTRAL PLANETS

The absence of a specific planetary trait may be reflected
in our physical appearance as much as the strength or a
specific trait.

Example: One individual was born with a strong
Jupiter and Moon whereas Saturn was neutral
(possesses no conditions or strength in the birth
map). Therefore, this person is inclined to be
chubby and round (Jupiter, Moon) and is definitely
not boney or thin (Saturn is non-prominent).

BEGINNER'S CHECKLIST

To construct your own Astro-Physical portrait, you will need a copy of your astrological birthmap, and possibly the assistance of someone knowledgeable in astrology.

1. What is your Moon Sign (*especially females*)?

   _____

2. What is your Sun Sign?

   _____

3. Are you born within two days of a cusp? If so, what is the neighboring sign?

   _____

4. Are you born near sunset or midnight? If so, then locate your Opposite Sun Sign by counting 180 days forward from your birth day. What sign does this date occur in?

   _____

5. What is your Ascendant Sign?

   _____

6. Does your Ascendant degree occur in the last 5° of a sign? If so, then what is the following sign?

   _____

7. What planet(s) are closest to your Ascendant degree?

   _____

8. In what sign is the planetary ruler of your Ascendant?

   _____

9. Is your Moon closely conjunct (allow an orb of 3°) any planet? If so, what planet? (Do not include the Sun.)

_____

10. Is your Sun closely conjunct (allow 5° orb) any planet? If so, what planet? (Do not include Mercury or Moon. Allow only 1° for the planet Venus.)

_____

11. Do you have any planets that are very strong by placement? (*See page 40.*) List these planets.

_____

12 Were your born when any planet was stationary? If so, what planet? (*See number 10, Table 2, page 36.*)

_____

13. Are at least two of the following: Sun, Moon, Ascendant sign found in any one of the four astrological elements? (*See page 15, "The Elements and Modes."*) What element?

_____

14. Are at least two of the following: Sun, Moon, Ascendant sign found in any one of the three astrological modes? (*See page 15, "The Elements and Modes."*) What mode?

_____

You may discover yourself to be a relatively pure astrological body type as described for any sign or planetary type occurring for points 1 – 8 of this checklist. Most likely you are a combination of two or three planetary, sign, elemental or (rare) modal types occurring for points 1 – 14.

CHART OF
PLANETARY DIGNITIES & DEBILITIES

Planetary Body	Rulership	Exaltation	Detriment	Fall
Sun	Leo	Aries	Aquarius	Libra
Moon	Cancer	Taurus	Capricorn	Scorpio
Mercury	Gemini/Virgo	Aquarius	Sagittarius/Pisces	Leo
Venus	Taurus/Libra	Pisces	Scorpio/Aries	Virgo
Mars	Aries/Scorpio	Capricorn	Libra/Taurus	Cancer
Jupiter	Sagittarius/Pisces	Cancer	Gemini/Virgo	Capricorn
Saturn	Capricorn/Aquarius	Libra	Cancer/Leo	Aries

Outer Planets

Note: The exaltation, detriment and fall positions of the three astrological outer-most planets (circa the year the book was written) are not yet determined with certainty.

Uranus	Aquarius	Scorpio	Leo	Taurus
Neptune	Pisces	Cancer	Virgo	Capricorn
Pluto	Scorpio	Aries	Taurus	Libra

THE ZODIACAL SIGN TYPES

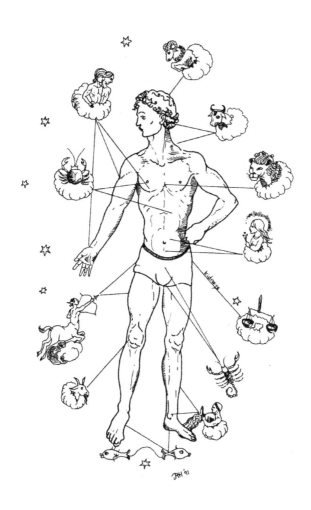

ARIES

Ruled by MARS (See page 125)
Element: FIRE; Mode: CARDINAL

CONSCIOUSNESS SYMBOLIZED
Spontaneous action, life force, birth, uninhibited energy.

EXPRESSES PHYSICALLY AS...
TYPE 1, Primary Type: See "Mars", page 125.

TYPE 2: The second Aries type is lean and has high cheekbones, an angular or narrow, pointed jaw line, a small, sharp and upturned or sharp and cat-like nose,* upward-slanting eyes, clearly outlined full red lips, red or blonde hair (in Caucasians), broad shoulders and narrow hips.

GENERAL COMMENTS
Both Aries types enjoy the color red. The second type is very common in Aries females and may indicate an admixture with the related fire sign Leo. Look for the widow's peak, strongly V-shaped or joined eyebrows and a bald spot or prominence towards the back crown of the head.

---

* *In some cases the nostrils are fully visible from frontal view, signaling an impulsive, reckless nature.*

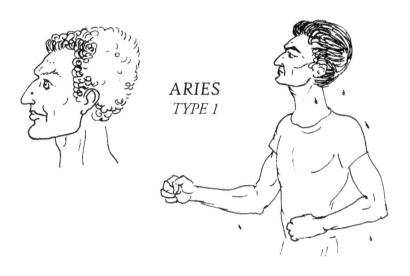

ARIES
TYPE 1

ARIES
TYPE 2

MANNER

The Aries type is energetic and spunky. They manifest a positive "Let's go!" quality; exuberant playfulness, or an an excess of irritable impatience. Aries folks like to accomplish their aims without undue delay. They evince a cheerfully ambitious manner and are somewhat unconscious of their effect on others around them.

Aries love to laugh. Playful, fun loving and vital, they are always game for a new experience or project. Aries like to carry out their goals and satisfy their urges NOW! Energy arises spontaneously in the muscles of this type. Therefore, Aries people require "sudden" walks, runs or other physical "safety valves" and dislike physical restraint. A positive, extroverted sign, yet fully capable of acting independently.

ARIES TYPE CAREERS

All careers requiring initiative, courage, creativity and assertiveness. Avoid boring, sedentary and routine careers or any strongly subordinate positions. Explorer, race car driver, lead singer, modern artist, athlete salesperson, teacher, musician, motivational speaker.

ARIES TYPE PROFILES
Eye, nose, eyebrows, top of head, hair are emphasized.

OVERVIEW

One in two Aries will evince traits of the classic Aries appearance. Be sure to also check the Moon's sign and the rising sign. Aries is a hybrid of Mars and Fire. Also consider the three Decanate modifications for Aries (*page 171*).

ARIES SIGNATURES:

- something striking or notable about the eyes, eyebrows, forehead or hair
- course hair, often red or blonde where pertinent
- back of head rising toward the crown
- nose either narrow and aquiline or upturned with nostrils exposed
- freckles, moles or scars on face
- very narrow/very wide jaw
- baldness in men
- widow's peaks (V-shaped hairline)
- energetic, cheerful manner
- lean, muscular
- fond of red
- flushed appearance
- a fairer sign for the gene pool
- sharp features, high cheekbones
- bright, upbeat or strident voice
- moderate height

Cheerfulness, positivity, zest for life, plus an exceptionally playful and adventuresome spirit are typical of Aries! As a Fire sign, Aries is prone to baldness.

TAURUS
Ruled by VENUS (See page 119)
Element: EARTH; Mode: FIXED

CONSCIOUSNESS SYMBOLIZED

Physical body and physical forms, beauty, nature, satisfaction, appetites of the flesh, contentment, stabilization of energy.

EXPRESSES PHYSICALLY AS...

The Taurean has a square and muscular, well-built frame. Taurus types have solid, heavy bones, and large, fleshy hands and feet. The face and jaw tend to be square with the lower face dominant. The mouth is very large and sensual; the chin is square and dimpled or cleft. Taurean noses are soft and wide, as is the general appearance of the face. The eyes are large-lidded, soft and "bovine" looking, as is the general expression.

Taurus hair is thick, soft and inclines to brown tones. When possible the eyes also tend toward a brown, earthy coloration. The neck and shoulders are very powerful and thick. Voice quality is outstanding in some way, and the Adam's apple may be prominent. Hearing, dental and vocal complaints are common to the type.

GENERAL COMMENTS

Taurus people enjoy well-made and textural clothing and are one of the best dressed of the Sign Types. The body is always very warm. This type is prone to excess weight through overeating. Defense football players are frequently of the Taurus physical

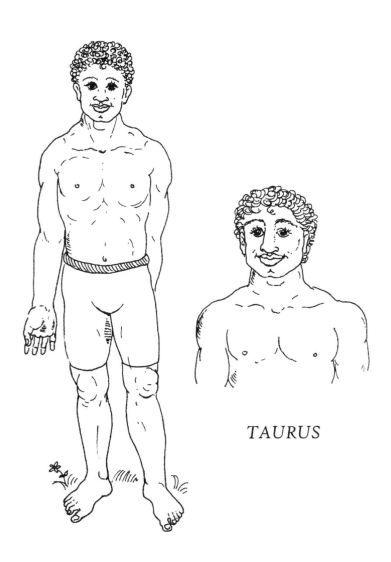

TAURUS

type. However, when mixed with a Virgo influence (*See page 171, Appendix 2, The 36 Decanates*), Taurus produces a petite yet well-formed body and a prettier, daintier face. Many Taurean women possess beautiful, full hour-glass figures, similar to Mae West, who had a Taurus Ascendant.

MANNER

The Taurus manner is calm and earthy. This is an unflappable sign, amiable and easy-going. The vibration is slow and steady, like the bovine species. Sexual magnetism is high.

TAURUS TYPE CAREERS

All careers requiring artistic talent, realism, practicality, steadiness and endurance. Avoid positions requiring excessive speed, flexibility or routine disruptions. Artist, chef, banker, jeweler or gem dealer, football player, treasurer, musician, gardener, builder, farmer, landscape designer, potter, realestate agent, designer, bricklayer, heavy equipment operator, produce and raw goods worker, manufacturer.

TAURUS

Large, padded, square hands and feet; full forehead; this sign rules ears and voice.

TAURUS
EARTH TYPE

TAURUS
VENUSIAN TYPE

OVERVIEW

One in two Taurus people will evince traits of a classic Taurus appearance. Be sure to also check the Moon's sign and the rising sign. Taurus is a hybrid of the Earth element, the Fixed mode, and the planet Venus. Also consider the three Decanate modifications for Taurus (*page 171*).

TAURUS SIGNATURES:

- full features, wide nostrils, full lips
- prominence or fullness of lower face, ears, mouth, jaw neck
- rich, pleasant and mellow, or magnetic voice —or a vocal defect
- square, solid body type (either lean or heavy)
- heavier bones than average
- square hands and feet
- full, soft, thick and beautiful hair (males tend to keep it!)
- full "bulging" forehead
- large, sometimes bulging eyes
- moderate height
- broad shoulders
- this type builds muscle easily
- women are buxom, and sometimes of hour-glass shape (curvy)
- great magnetic projection, sexy
- good appetites!
- warm bodied, warm hands
- large or square well-padded hands

GEMINI
Ruled by MERCURY (See page 114)
Element: AIR; Mode: MUTABLE

IMPORTANT NOTES FOR ALL GEMINI TYPES

Watch for expressive hands, and/or multiple finger rings or bracelets. Geminis are noted for their beautiful, luminous and elfin-like twinkling eyes. The true Gemini type is quick moving, agile and surprisingly strong despite a slender or lanky appearance.

The shoulders, while not muscular, are sometimes quite broad, giving a "coat hanger" appearance to the upper frame, and the neck is long and narrow. This is a long legged and a slim hipped sign, with a high positioned *gluteus maximus*, similar to opposite sign Sagittarius. The forehead is also high, with a noticeable upper portion. The sign tends toward fine hair and the males to frontal baldness. (*Also see "Air", page 24.*)

The general impression is sparkling, merrily witty, if not sarcastic, and they rarely stop talking! Often, you find Gemini carting along the accoutrements of their latest hobby: a camera, ski poles, a favorite new book, roller skates or odd gadgets. This sign delights in "personal" transportation such as motorbikes, bicycles, roller blades and skateboards.

CONSCIOUSNESS SYMBOLIZED

Self-coordination, communication, duality, speech

EXPRESSES PHYSICALLY AS...

TYPE 1, Primary Type: See "Mercury", page 114.

TYPE 2: Very tall, high-waisted and thin-bodied, often athletic, the Type 2 Gemini often looks emaciated. The nose is long and aquiline and the mouth is small and thin-lipped, giving one the strong impression of a bird. The forehead of this type is very high, with eyes somewhat pop-eyed in expression and set wide apart (a feature common to all three Air signs).

GENERAL COMMENTS

Gemini hair is peculiarly fine, flyaway, and wavy, tending to be light brown in the Caucasian type. The hands and arms are long, thin and noticeable. This is a high-waisted sign, with legs much longer than the torso. Geminis often have one wandering eye or an uncoordinated frontal gaze. Geminians are noted for their luminous, highly expressive, sometimes beautiful and definitely twinkling eyes. Shoulders are broad or "Egyptian."

MANNER

TYPE 1, Primary Type: See "Mercury", page 114.

TYPE 2: This type seems very restless and ill-at-ease, as if driven by scattered and over-worked thoughts. They almost always smoke too much and eat poorly. This type is mentally deeper than the Type 1 Gemini and loves to investigate various topics. They are typically knowledgeable and open to philosophical or political discussions, and they love to play the devil's advocate. Stability (financial or otherwise) seems to elude this type and they are commonly found among rock musicians, writers and drifters.

GEMINI TYPE CAREERS

All careers demanding dexterity, versatility, communication, quickness. Avoid positions of authority, or those requiring a long attention span and follow-through. Reporter, messenger, writer,

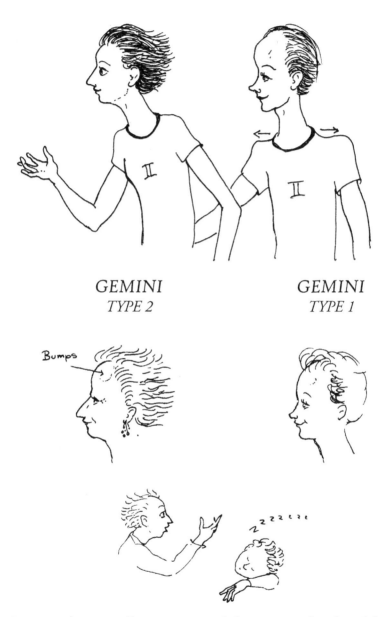

GEMINI
TYPE 2

GEMINI
TYPE 1

Gemini is the most talkative sign! Watch for expressive hands and face.

juggler, magician, postal carrier, lawyer, taxi driver, jack of all trades, waiter, porter, telephone operator, toy-maker, traveling entertainer, comedian, translator, multi-linguistic, drummer, flautist, columnist, songwriter, ski and tennis instructor.

OVERVIEW

One in two Geminians will evince traits classic to Gemini. Be sure to also check the Moon's sign and the rising sign. Gemini is a hybrid of the Air element, the Mutable mode and the planet Mercury. Also consider the three Decanate modifications for Gemini (*page 171*).

GEMINI SIGNATURES:

- high voice, chattering, talkative
- large, luminous and sparkling eyes,
  even pop-eyed expression
- delicate skin
- pointed chin; pointed, thin beard
  and carefully groomed mustache
- thin, fine hair, usually straight (males bald)
- dainty, pixie features *(See "Mercury", page 114)*
  or aquiline, bird-like features
- hands and arms are notable in some way (too large,
  gesticulating constantly, rings, etc.)
- broad shoulders and non-muscular chest
- body type is either elfin, agile, spry and small (Mercurial) or
  long boned, lanky, non-muscular
  with very long legs (high waisted)
- "coat hanger" shoulders, narrow hips
- friendly, energetic, chipper, fun-loving, mischievous, curious,
  scattered, and sometimes nervous
- many Geminis enjoy fun experimental exercise like
  skateboarding, skiing, motorcycling, or parkour

CANCER
Ruled by MOON (See page 109)
Element: WATER; Mode: CARDINAL

CONSCIOUSNESS SYMBOLIZED

Awareness of the internal environment, personal feelings, subjective emotional states. Protection of self and others.

GENERAL COMMENTS

The primary type Cancerian exactly resembles the Lunar type. The classic Moon or Lunar type appears to be fashioned after the Moon in her FULL phase, whereas the Type 2 Cancerian reflects the New Moon. This is an important distinction, as the two types are very different in face, physical form, and psychology.

EXPRESSES PHYSICALLY AS...

TYPE 1, Primary Full Moon Type: See "Moon", page 109.

TYPE 2, Secondary New Moon Type: The New Moon Cancerian has a long, narrow face with a sad, dreamy and somewhat woebegone expression. On first glance the New Moon Cancerian has much in common with the Saturnian type. However, a deeper observation will reveal that this type possesses none of the Saturnian's brittleness. The body is narrow, especially at the chest and shoulders, which appear exceedingly delicate and "birdboned." The body is graceful and fluid. When youthful, the body is slender to emaciated, yet, with age, may put on considerable watery weight. The nose is long and aquiline, the eyes large and sad. The mouth is long and fine and the jaw quite narrow.

The hair of the New Moon Cancerian is often abundant, wavy and worn very long. Dark coloration seems more typical than fair. The complexion and attractiveness vary depending on the day, mood or light. This type can be hauntingly beautiful one day and quite plain the next. The hands are delicate and sensitive with conical to pointed finger tips. The overall look is that of "The High Priestess" seen in the Major Arcana of the Waite and Ryder Tarot decks.

MANNER

TYPE 1, Primary Full Moon Type: See "Moon," page 109.

TYPE 2: Once again, the Type 2, or New Moon Cancerian is very different from her sister, the Type 1 or Full Moon Cancerian. The New Moon Cancerian's manner is elusive and evasive. The air about her is pensive and sad. Seemingly remote, she prefers solitude and is greatly addicted to literature and novels. She is poetic, magnetic, psychic and musical. New Moon Cancerians are greatly prone to depression and seem to lack the normal will to live. Exceedingly sensitive they shun both the Sun's rays and the active work-day world, loving the night. This can be a deeply spiritual type, lacking much of the "common-touch" and matronly qualities of the more common Full Moon Type Cancerian. Frequently, the New Moon Cancerian lives in her own mental world of romance and fantasy.

CANCER TYPE CAREERS

All careers of a domestic, personal and nurturing nature. Home business suits Cancers well. Mother, nurse, cook, gardener, interior decorator, curator, doll maker, antique dealer, dog and cat care, shopkeeper, caretaker, office organizer, small business operator, child-care worker, tutor, dancer, genealogist, potter, family therapist, animal farmer, shepherd, historian, novelist, poet, musician, tarot reader.

OVERVIEW

One in two Cancerians will evince traits classic to their sign. Be sure to also check the Moon sign and the rising sign. Cancer is a hybrid of the Water element and the Moon. Also consider the three Decanate modifications for Cancer (*page 171*).

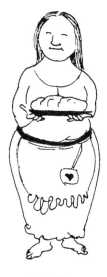

CANCER
*TYPE 1 ***
(FULL MOON)

CANCER
TYPE 2
(NEW MOON)

CANCER SIGNATURES:

Full Moon Type:

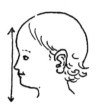

- round, flat face, weak bone structure
- deep set eyes
- weak chin
- small "slit" mouth or large, full lips
- round or phlegmatic body (*See "Water," pg 18*)
- small shoulders
- females are buxom
- protruding stomach
- very small hands and feet
- round hairline
- abundant hair worn long
- males keep their hair
- often musical
- emotionally intimate and nurturing

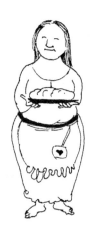

New Moon Type:

- frail, sensitive body, often quite slender
- big sad eyes, long narrow face
- very small or very large mouth
- weak chin
- females are flat chested
- delicate hands and feet, often small
- hair often abundant, worn long
- depressive atmosphere
- loves to read
- often musical
- emotionally intimate, poetic, and shy

LEO

Ruled by SUN (See page 104)
Element: FIRE; Mode: FIXED

CONSCIOUSNESS SYMBOLIZED

Self as God, ego, mastery, will, pleasure, self as center; the creative principle individualized.

EXPRESSES PHYSICALLY AS...

The Leo type has a broad, angular face, very high cheekbones and a cat-like face with beautifully large upwardly-slanting eyes that have a confident and haughty gaze. The nose is sharply outlined and has characteristically flared, cat-like nostrils. The full lips are sharply outlined and the upper lip curls or sneers in the manner of Elvis Presley. The head is large and the chin pronounced. The jawline is firm. The Leonian body is of medium height with very broad shoulders and narrow hips. Arms, back and chest are muscular and well-developed.

The Leo body temperature is warm, and the complexion and hands may appear flushed. Age may witness the arrival of deep jowls and sweeping folds of skin from nose flange to outer corner of mouth. Leo native Alfred Hitchcock provides the best example of this effect. Leos are famous for their full and striking "manes" of hair with strong color (any color). The voice is low and very strong, sometimes authoritative. Leos dress in a loud or gaudy manner, love garish jewelry, especially gold medallions and emblems worn about the upper chest. This is a healthy, strong, vital and extremely handsome type.

LEO

MANNER

Confident, warm and haughty, Leos appear remarkably composed yet simultaneously vital and passionate. True Leos have stage-presence anywhere and are able to project force and magnetism. Mae West, Mick Jagger and Madonna are excellent examples.

LEO TYPE CAREERS

All careers requiring management, authority, dash and style. Avoid non-creative, boring or background positions. Art and theater director, film director or producer, playground or park director, coach, actor, manager, boss, entrepreneur, stockbroker, youth worker, professional gambler, advertising talent agent, resort personnel, firefighter, band leader, forest ranger, sales.

OVERVIEW

One in two Leos will evince traits classic to their sign. Be sure to also check the Moon's sign and the rising sign. Also consider the three Decanate modifications for Leo (*See page 171*).

LEO

LEO SIGNATURES:
- large head
- big chin or jaw
- high cheekbones
- flaring nostrils
- full, but sneering upper lip
- males tend to bald
- full, gorgeous hair in females, often wavy or curling
- very broad shoulders, strong backs and narrow hips
- lean thighs
- powerful energy
- strong, authoritative voices
- muscular
- jowls develop later in life
- proud and playful manner
- dresses to attract attention
- enjoys bright colors
- gorgeous or handsome

In later years, heavy folds and jowls
show pride and fondness
for power. Male Leo types tend
toward top and frontal balding.

VIRGO
Ruled by MERCURY (See page 114)
Element: EARTH; Mode: MUTABLE

CONSCIOUSNESS SYMBOLIZED

The discriminative intellect; the perfection and preparation of the material plane or body; detail, service, humility, boundary-making.

EXPRESSES PHYSICALLY AS...

See "Mercury," p. 114, for primary type. Also see "Earth" type, p. 20, as the occasional Virgo type appears more Earthy than Mercurial.

GENERAL COMMENTS

The Virgo type is either exceedingly tidy and tasteful or quite the reverse. Natives of this sign frequently resemble their opposite sign, Pisces, so be prepared to encounter frequent "Piscean" Virgos. The hair suffers in this sign—premature grayness, dry-ness, lack of body and drab color seems rather typical. The body is also dry and prone to dehydration and facial lining. The extreme Virgo nose may appear narrow and pinched as if an invisible clothespin had been applied. Normally a fit, agile and petite sign, when mixed with Taurus, Jupiter or Neptune, this type may be tank-like and somewhat clumsy.

MANNER

This sign is of modest reserve, quick alert, and efficient. Virgos are always busy about something, unlike the other Mercurial sign, Gemini. The manner is pragmatic yet cheerful, and the wit is as

VIRGO

VIRGO
MERCURIAL TYPE

VIRGO
EARTH TYPE

sharp as a knife. Virgos dislike being idle and will even combine socializing time with shopping or other errands. Preoccupation with health, clothing or chores is typical.

VIRGO TYPE CAREERS

All careers requiring patience, exactitude, speed, detail and order. Avoid high-profile positions or those requiring intuition and creativity. Secretary, nurse, administrator, file clerk, typist, psychologist, typesetter, dental and medical assistant, social worker, veterinarian, farmer, beekeeper, printer, seamstress, clothing manufacturing and salesperson, accountant, statistician, word processor, court reporter, object repair person, mechanic, therapist, mid-wife, homeopath, market analyst, crafts-person, cartographer, technical illustrator drafts-person.

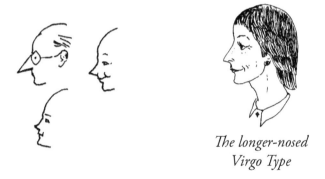

*The longer-nosed
Virgo Type*

Virgo noses are sharp and narrow! Long, very thin lips are also Virgo trademarks. Watch for an observant, practical and sharp mind. The best listeners are Virgos.

OVERVIEW

One in two Virgos will evince traits classic to Virgo. Be sure to also check the Moon sign and rising sign. Virgo is a hybrid of Mercury, the Earth Element and the Mutable Mode. All types exist, as well as the three Decanate modifications for Virgo *(see page 171)*.

VIRGO SIGNATURES:

- refined, finely cut facial features
- long, thin lips with points at corners
- long, thin, narrow, pointy noses (relative to the gene pool)
- fit, agile, slender body type, wiry, on shorter side of the family gene pool.
- males and females both are of the "gymnast" type.
- occasional Virgos are more Earthy, than Mercurial *(See "Earth," page 20)*
- fast moving, alert, reserved, intelligent, efficient
- often shy
- high, fast voices
- thin, fine hair, typically quite straight (where gene pool allows), kept short and neat
- prone to premature greying, dandruff, dry skin
- loves clothes; tasteful dresser, pays careful attention to personal appearance
- small hands
- small head (in Mercury type)
- reserved
- busy!

LIBRA
Ruled by VENUS (See page 119)
Element: AIR; Mode: CARDINAL

CONSCIOUSNESS SYMBOLIZED

Balance, cooperation, compromise,
justice, observation, relaxation.

EXPRESSES PHYSICALLY AS...

See "Venus," page 119.

GENERAL COMMENTS

In Libra, the Venusian expression is quite pure. Typical Libran attributes are the egg-shaped, oval head and face, although occasionally Libra gives a round face. The forehead and upper head are high and full, whereas the jaw is quite weak and the chin may be entirely lacking. True Librans almost always have lovely voices. Some astrologers note a secondary Libra type said to exactly resemble an owl. Many Librans possess small sweet features and a "baby-face" look.

MANNER

See Venus, page 119. The manner is elegant, courtly, polite and very friendly.

Venusian
"Baby-faced"
Libran

LIBRA
TYPES

"Owl" Libran

LIBRA TYPE CAREERS

All careers requiring charm, reasoning power, social grace and diplomacy. Librans love one-to-one discussion. Diplomat, lawyer, receptionist, TV and radio host, librarian, interviewer, art or theater agent for artist and so on, partner, pilot, judge, chairperson, consultant of any kind, psychologist, model, mediator. Surprisingly, many great generals have been born under this sign. Avoid vocations that get you physically dirty, deal exclusively with objects (unless beautiful ones), or are isolated and silent.

One of the more common body types for female Libras is full chest, pretty face, flat bottom, narrow hips, long slender legs, long, narrow hands and feet.

OVERVIEW

One in two Librans will evince traits classic to Libra. Be sure to also check the Moon sign and the rising sign. Libra is a hybrid of the Air Element and the planet Venus. All types exist as well as the three Libra Decanate modifications *(See page 171).*

LIBRA SIGNATURES:

- beautiful, sweet face or "baby-faced"
- full eyelids, pretty eyes
- oval face
- charming voice
- gracefully formed mouth with
  "Cupid's bow" look to upper lip
- petite, dainty, or tiny nose / or well formed
   moderate and curved nose—sometimes the female
   nose is too small
- lovely, moist, shiny hair (males tend to baldness)
- moderate height, graceful body, usually slender
- long, narrow hands and feet
- long legs
- females often have "flat" behinds and full chests
- sometimes an androgynous sign for males
- occasional Librans remind one of an owl:
   long nose, scholarly appearance and
   thoughtful, intelligent manner
- weak chin
- smooth, lovely and velvety skin / or acne

SCORPIO
Ruled by MARS & PLUTO (See pages 125 & 150)
Element: WATER; Mode: FIXED

CONSCIOUSNESS SYMBOLIZED

Power and knowledge over the physical world, strategizing, manipulation of energy, sex, death and rebirth, regeneration, concentration of emotion.

EXPRESSES PHYSICALLY AS...

The body is of short to medium stature with a very strong gaze and thick-set frame. The limbs are dense and heavy. Scorpio gives denseness to the hair as well, this being one of the most hirsute types. Coloration is prone towards darkness: black, if this is genetically possible, or red. The hair is course in texture, as is the skin which is all too frequently pocked, scared, or prone to severe acne. Scorpio governs the sweat glands, and the pores of the skin are very large. Body odor is strong. Listen for the trademark low, sultry or sexy "smoker's" voice. There seem to exist two very distinct facial types.

FACIAL TYPE 1

The first facial type has very fine "cut" or chiseled features, large fine, sharp or beaked nose. The complexion runs to extremes such as snow-white skin, red lips and black hair. This type resembles an eagle. The women of this type are icily beautiful and very seductive. Look for red or black clothing, spike heels and long red nails. The eyes of this type are keen and cool of expression and project an intensity rarely found in other signs.

FACIAL TYPE 2 – See Pluto, page 150.

The second facial type has crude, thick, heavy features. Scorpio noses are large or noticeable in some way, i.e. broken, cleft, blunted (Scorpio rules the nose). The lips of this type are thick, heavy, red and, sometimes, unpleasantly formed. Scorpios of this type usually have "beetle brows," or give the appearance of peering out from under or behind something. The facial expression is deadpan and the mood hard to read. The head is square, the face full, and the body, thick and paunchy. This is one of the zodiac's physically strongest and most resilient types.

MANNER

The Scorpio has a penetrating and deliberate manner. Their psychic atmosphere is unusually intense, and the concentration of reserved emotional and physical force is perhaps the greatest of any sign. The face is generally not very expressive unless Pisces, Aries, Sagittarius, or perhaps Gemini are present. Scorpio is characteristically a secretive and self-witholding sign. Feel for an aura of great brooding intensity. The manner is never happy, silly, jolly, light-hearted or gay.

SCORPIO TYPE CAREERS

Scorpio types excel at careers of intensity, power, danger, specialization, and the manipulation or analysis of resources, objects and people. Avoid wide focus, low impact positions.

Investigator, detective, researcher, doctor, surgeon, archaeologist, chemist, prostitute, recycler, waste manager, embalmer, insurance agent, banker, psychologist, geneticist, psychic, professional chess player, strategist, FBI or CIA agent, lawyer, physicist, banker, plumber, military general, real estate manager and appraiser, epidemiologist, biologist.

TYPE 1
"The Eagle"

SCORPIO
TYPES

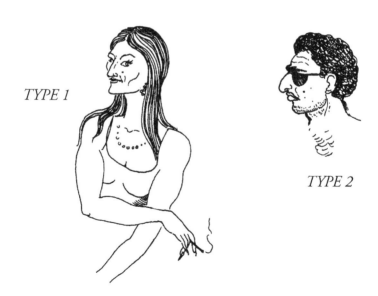

TYPE 1

TYPE 2

OVERVIEW

One in two Scorpio people will evince traits of a classic Scorpio appearance. Be sure to also check the Moon sign and the rising sign. Scorpio is a hybrid of the Water element, the Fixed mode, and the planets Mars and Pluto. Check the three Scorpio Decanate modifications *(See page 171)*.

SCORPIO SIGNATURES:

- dense hair, intense colors
- eyebrows joined or V-shaped
- high contrast between skin/hair/eyes
- something "funny" or outstanding about the nose: beaked, hooked, broken or large nose
- low, sexy, or "smoker's" voice–a Scorpio give away!
- very chiseled lips, or very heavy, unchiseled lips
- intense, fierce expression (think of an eagle)
- smoldering, hypnotic beauty
- low forehead, widow's peak
- moles, scars, acne
- hirsute
- dense bones, stong!
- compressed, tightly drawn upper lip
- heavy face and square chin in Type 2
- mood is either a serious deadpan or a "brewing and stewing"
- high energy and stamina
- projects controlled power
- intense and sexy

SAGITTARIUS
Ruled by JUPITER (See page 131)
Element: FIRE; Mode: MUTABLE

CONSCIOUSNESS SYMBOLIZED

Self-expansion, broadening of horizons, independence, free will, questing, growth of the higher mind, knowledge.

EXPRESSES PHYSICALLY AS...

SAGITTARIUS TYPE 1 – *Primary Type*

Sagittarian types possess a medium to tall body with long limbs. Some types are muscular and athletic in appearance, whereas others have a lanky, loose-jointed and gangly look. The Sagittarian type has very long legs, strong thighs and buttocks and is narrow-hipped when viewed frontally. When viewed from the side, the buttocks are full and protruding. Typical Sagittarian heads are long and narrow. The hair is straight, free flowing and brown. the nose is long and straight; the mouth very broad with large teeth, Sagittarian eyes are large and alert, possessing a strong fiery quality. The neck is long and slender, and the overall appearance is "horsey." The legs are often beautifully formed, though sometimes quite slender, especially at the ankle and calf.

SAGITTARIUS TYPE 2 – *Secondary Type*

See "Jupiter," page 131.

SAGITTARIUS
TYPE 1
The "Horsey" Type

SAGITTARIUS
TYPE 2
Jupiterian Type

MANNER

This Sagittarian sign type possesses a highly positive auric field. The manner is hyperactive, enthused and impatient. Sagittarians appear extremely eager as if ready to jump up and try anything. This is a nervous, fidgety sign that does not like to sit still. Sagittarians are talkative, friendly, and enlivening. This is perhaps the most truly vivacious of all sign types. Hand gestures are full and generous, the laugh full, and the walk strident.

TYPE CAREERS

All careers requiring an outgoing, enthusiastic, energetic and positive nature. Avoid dull, sedentary positions requiring accuracy and detail; freedom is essential. Advertiser, import-exporter, international worker of many kinds, teacher, orchestra conductor, pilot, train engineer, traveling salesperson, publicist and promoter, international networker and communicator, gambler, explorer, baseball player, track and field star, sportsman, truck driver, tour guide, expedition leader, preacher, public speaker, surveyor, astronaut (unless hyperactive).

OVERVIEW

One in two Sagittarian people will evince traits of a classic Sagittarius appearance. Be sure to also check the Moon sign and the rising sign. Sagittarius is a hybrid of the Fire element, the Mutable mode and Jupiter. Three or four types exist, as well as the three Sagittarian Decanate modifications *(See page 171)*.

SAGITTARIUS SIGNATURES:

The "Horsey" Type:
- the taller, narrower end of the available gene pool
- lanky build, long limbs (excellent runners
  and baseball players!)
- long attractive legs, high hips and high waisted,
  sometimes the buttocks protrude backward
  (this sign rules the hips and thighs)
- athletic, muscular and energetic, full of "viv" and vigor
- restless, energized, enthusiastic, positive and often hyper
- large, broad friendly smile with large teeth,
  medium to fine lips
- features are often larger than face but not unpleasantly so
- long, straight or slightly aquiline nose, pleasantly formed
- long, narrow face, with large, alert and sparkling eyes
- intelligent look, loud laugh, positive vocal tone
- positive manner: cheerful, generous and encouraging to all
- enjoys wearing bright colors and athletic style clothing
- hair often long and straight (think of horse's mane),
  typically worn free flowing

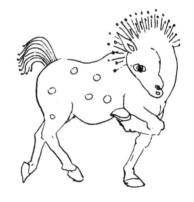

The Jupiterian Type:
See Jupiter: page 131

CAPRICORN
Ruled by SATURN (See page 137)
Element: EARTH; Mode: CARDINAL

CONSCIOUSNESS SYMBOLIZED

Control of the outer environment, achievement, perfection of goals.

EXPRESSES PHYSICALLY AS...

TYPE 1 – THE SATURNIAN CAPRICORN
(See "Saturn," page 137).

The nose need not be long or hooked in every case. Capricornian women of the Saturnian type are often exceptionally beautiful examples of the chiseled type. Both sexes dress tastefully and possess an air of cool dignity.

TYPE 2 – THE EARTHY CAPRICORN

The head is large and distinctly round and hard, possessing firm jaws. Facial features are petite and well-formed. The mouth is small and tight, with the lips hardly evident. The face may appear somewhat flat in profile, and the eyes are small and deep-set. The torso is large and tank-like with an abundance of either hard fat or muscle covered with a layer of hard fat. Upper arms are noticeably thick, although the shoulders are not wide and may incline to slope.

Physical motion is slow and steady, and the type is unflappable in danger. A large belly often protrudes below. Hands and feet are large, thickset and heavy. This type bears a lot in common with its opposite Sun sign, Cancer (Type 1, Full Moon Cancerian). However, the Type 2 Capricornian is larger, stronger and firmer of flesh than the Full Moon Cancerian, and the biceps, hands and

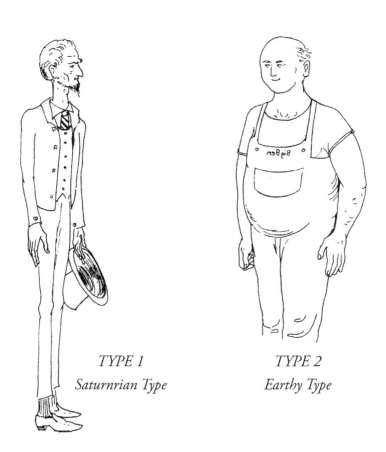

TYPE 1
Saturnrian Type

TYPE 2
Earthy Type

CAPRICORN
TYPES

feet are much meatier than those found among Cancerians. This Type produces the well-loved patriarch or matriarch and makes excellent politicians, police officers, business persons, grocers, heavyweight boxers, and bakers.

TYPE 3 CAPRICORN

This common physical expression of Capricorn, seldom recorded, is seen over and over again. The head is squarish, with a somewhat flat overall appearance. Facial features are small and clean-cut. The mouth is narrow and the lips exceedingly fine. Jawline and chin are set firm and squared. The nose is small and refined, yet never pixie-like. An overall impression of cuteness is ruined by the serious, firm and determined set of the features and expression. This is a handsome, clean-lined type. The hair of this third Capricornian type is usually very straight, think, brown and worn short and neatly cut. The skin is very fine and very fair in Caucasians.

CAPRICORNIAN BODY TYPES

1. The heavyweight boxer type, built like a tank throughout.
2. The elegantly petite type. These people are quite dignified and hold themselves in perfect posture. The body is well balanced, graceful, yet prone to stiffness. The legs are short, unlike Types 1 and 3.
3. The Saturnian body *(See "Saturn")*. Both Type 1 and 2 Capricornian facial types can combine with the Saturnian body type.

GENERAL COMMENTS

Capricorn rules the knees. Watch for the characteristically Capricornian knobby, protruding knees. All Capricornian types seem to posses remarkable stamina and muscular strength.

CAPRICORN
TYPE 3

MANNER

Capricornian Types are deliberate, focused and dignified in manner. The appearance is in all ways professional. The impression is both serious—and sincere. The vibrational atmosphere is cool, although the Type 2, Earthy Capricorn is somewhat warmer. Self-composure, dignity and great earnestness are hallmarks of the sign. Capricorn actress Marlene Dietrich gives a perfect example of this sign's cool dignity.

CAPRICORN TYPE CAREERS

Capricorns are best in positions where advancement and organizational control is possible. Avoid standstill positions or those requiring emotional sensitivity. Corporate president, capitalist, land developer, business person, government official, administrator, dean, building contractor, architect, doctor, graphic artist, cartographer, top bureaucrat, mathematician, marketing director, furniture businessman, hardware and building supplier, manufacturer, police worker, land manager, landscaper.

OVERVIEW

One in two Capricorn people will evince traits of a classic Capricornian appearance. Be sure to also check the Moon sign and the rising sign. Capricorn is a hybrid of Saturn and Earth. Both types exist, plus the three Capricorn Decanate modifications *(See page 171).*

CAPRICORN SIGNATURES:

The Saturnian Type:
a classic ectomorph, with:
• small head
• strong jaw line,
• small or fine-lipped mouth
• bleating sound in voice
• refined, well proportioned features,
  clean looks
• dignified, reserved, sometimes a
  quietly authoritative manner
• determined expression, strong will
• tasteful dress: simple yet elegant
• long fingers with prominent joints
• narrow, lean with large, knotty joints
• knobby knees
• strong bones, and strong!
• skin, nail and gum problems are
  common
• some types possess a flat-faced,
  "cute" featured appearance with
  a very square jaw

The Earthy Type:
See Earth, page 20

Saturnian Type
Capricorn

Saturnrian Type Capricorns
can be elegant, dignified, cool and tasteful.

AQUARIUS

Ruled by Saturn & Uranus (see pages 137 & 144)
Element: Air; Mode: Fixed

CONSCIOUSNESS SYMBOLIZED

Individuated (non-tribal) humanity, awareness of one's eternal self, awareness of the evolution of humanity, mental creativity, contribution to humanity, eclectic development, invention platonic love.

EXPRESSES PHYSICALLY AS...

Aquarius is the tallest of zodiac types. The appearance tends to be androgynous in manner and appearance (especially in females), yet unaffected. Aquarian types frequently are undeveloped in the upper body, with good muscular development in the lower body. The limbs are long and lanky, and the ankles noticeable in some way. "Piano legs," varicose veins, or very elongated shins and ankles are common.

The neck is long, and the large head may seem to float, similar to a balloon on a string. Some astrologers report that the Aquarian type is prone to buck teeth or overbites. All Aquarian types tend to have very high foreheads. Aquarian hair is softly waving, lovely unmanageable and of an extremely fine texture. Aquarius is one of the fairest of signs, relative to the individual's gene-pool. Many Aquarians show the perfect posture of their fellow Saturnians, the Capricorns. However, in the Aquarian, the body often seems mismatched, and the posture and gait appear awkward. This, of course, is not true in every case. Saturn influenced Aquarians stand conspicuously tall and straight.

There seem to be three distinct Aquarian facial types. Perhaps this is due to Decanate influence *(See Decanates, page 171)*.

Two body types:
Air (see page 24)
and rarely, Fixed (see page 20)

AQUARIUS

The tallest zodiac type
with lengthy shin bones

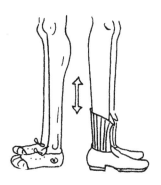

FACIAL TYPES

THE VENUSIAN AQUARIAN: The hallmark of this facial type is an extremely high, straight forehead, with wide-set, startlingly blue (when possible) eyes. The forehead may dominate the face. The overall expression is kindly, intelligent yet far-away looking.

The facial features and manner take on much of the Libran type (combined with the Aquarian). The lips are medium to full and the expression is pleasant and mild. Voices of this type may have an angelic, bell-like ring and full tone. All Aquarian types make wonderful orators. Hair and skin tend to be the fairest available in the native's gene-pool, and the hair is either fly-away and frizzy or very blonde and curly, both types of hair being unmanageable. In manner they are good-natured, kindly and highly intelligent. Unfailingly, this type possess some remarkable (though often little used) genius or inventive capacity. This type really does seem angelic and is usually quite eccentric, as are all Aquarian types.

THE SATURNIAN AQUARIAN: Abraham Lincoln is a prime example of this type, which shares much with the Saturnian type, although there are some notable departures. First, the face is rarely as cleanly cut as the true Saturnian, retaining all dignity, yet unique and less symmetrical. Not infrequently the outer angle of the eyelid is angled downward, indicative of wisdom. Additionally, the overall appearance is lanky and ungainly, lacking much of the dignified poise of true Saturnians.

These types are very unusual examples of humanity and always appear to others as eccentric or different from their fellows. Their expression is characteristically solemn,profoundly intelligent, yet punctuated with broad laughter and superlative wit. Predictably, they are geniuses. Perhaps this is one of the mentally deepest of all types, combining the depth of Saturn with the breadth, inspiration and vision of Aquarius. Frequently, they stand alone in life, yet may work for a greater good.

THE MERCURIAL AQUARIAN: This third Aquarian facial type is noted for beautiful classic pro-files, refined and clean cut features with a lovely, though some-times sad countenance. The young author, Virginia Woolf, was a perfect example of this type, as was Ronald Regam. The overall face and look is often remarkably well-balanced, refined and noble.

Ancient astrologers made Aquarius one of the three "Signs of Pulchritude" or physical beauty. [The three traditional "Signs of Pulchritude" are Aquarius, Leo and Libra. However, all signs produce beautiful types.] This type seemed much favored for male leads in Hollywood's golden era.

Note: It is possible that what the author designates here as the Mercurial Aquarian may be a second, more refined expression of the Saturnian Aquarian.

MANNER

There will always be something "a little different" about these types. Aquarians are very genuine and completely unpretentious. With the exception perhaps of the Saturnian-Aquarian, this type is extremely friendly and accepting. The eye holds a "hail-fellow-well-met" twinkle of friendliness towards all, and almost everyone feels welcomed by natives of this sign wherein platonic love is well-developed.

People of this sign type can appear extremely air-headed and remote and drift about like the head is leading the body, distracted and unaware of their surroundings. They may look past or through you when they shake your hand and are much better with groups than individuals, with ideas than realities.

AQUARIUS

Venusian /
Aquarian Type

Mercurial /
Aquarian Type

Venusian /
Aquarian Type

The noble Saturnian
Aquarian—
this Aquarian is a
Saturnian with a
pleasant expression.

These Aquarian types match the three planetary "decan"
rulers of Aquarius (Table 4, p. 171), plus Uranus and
the influence of the Air element.

The more Saturn influenced Aquarians are rather grave and earnest with deeply studious intellects. Their auras are cool, sad and remote. Venus-influenced Aquarians are pleasant, friendly and very nice people. In fact, you will be hard-pressed to find a truly dishonest, mean or unpleasant Aquarian. All Aquarian types possess a good sense of humor and a well-developed sense of the absurd. Uranus has much to do with electricity and seems to impart its electrical energy to the Aquarian aura. Many Aquarians possess a sort of electrical atmosphere, well-loved by audiences but a bit distancing up close. The impersonal manner of Aquarians is their hallmark.

GENERAL COMMENTS

The Aquarian manner of dress is quite interesting and unique. This type is very original in its manner of dress, yet rarely is preoccupied with vanities. Bright colors, mismatched patterns and materials, and remarkable hair styles can all be expected. Some of the women of this sign enjoy shocking people and attracting attention (Leo as opposite Sign), whereas the men seem to neglect themselves. Turquoise, purple and violet are often their favorite colors. Outmoded, peculiar or futuristic fashions and an altogether individualistic appearance are typical.

AQUARIUS TYPE CAREERS

Aquarius types excel at any inventive, futuristic or philanthropic occupation. Beware of overly conservative, non-individualistic or capitalistic positions, as well as jobs requiring extreme order or timeliness. Teacher, sports coach, philanthropist, peace corps worker, lecturer, inventor, electrician, congress person, senator, idea person, anthropologist, cartoonist, astrologer, scholar, beach or ski bum, union leader, activist, pilot, aviator, volunteer, scientist, astronomer, boat builder, high tech sports, photojournalist, jazz musician.

OVERVIEW

One in two Aquarian people will evince traits of a classic Aquarian appearance. Be sure to also check the Moon's sign and the rising sign. Aquarius is a hybrid of the Air element, Fixed mode and planets Saturn and Uranus. All types exist, plus the three Aquarian Decanate modifications *(See page 171).*

AQUARIUS SIGNATURES:

- one of the tallest signs (relevant to the available gene pool)
- oval face, pleasant, friendly but sincere and genuine manner
- moderate to large eyes are often set far apart
- look for downward slanting outer eye angle or outer eyelid position
- overbites and buck teeth
- big smiles, full frontal teeth
- huge foreheads, nicely domed heads
- fine, "flyaway" or frizzy hair, difficult to control.
- tends toward the blonde end of the available gene pool
- watch for very long shin bones
- beautiful "bell like" voice; intelligent voice
- beautiful, well balanced profile, often quite handsome
- females are small breasted
- lower body is stronger or heavier then upper body
- upper body may be weak
- many Aquarian women are somewhat androgynous
- watch for very odd or individualistic dressing style
- loves violet, purple, aqua and turquoise colors
- sense of humor
- intellectual or genius
- sometimes an androgynous sign for females

PISCES
Ruled by Jupiter & Neptune (See pages 131 & 147)
Element: Water; Mode: Mutable

CONSCIOUSNESS SYMBOLIZED

Universal love, selflessness, loss-of-boundaries, oneness, universality, escape from entrapment in matter, dissolution.

EXPRESSES PHYSICALLY AS...

Three very distinct Piscean types are outlined below:

TYPE 1 PISCEAN

A classic Piscean closely resembles a fish, possessing very large bulging or protruding eyes, large loose lips, weak facial bones and a loped forehead and chin. The head and body are round and usually plump. This one of the zodiac's shortest and roundest types, and also one of its sweetest. Their eyes merrily twinkle with sympathy and love. All of the facial features may appear too large, or somehow rubbery, elastic or ill-defined. The nose is soft and may have the characteristically Piscean "clown's" tip—or slightly upturned or bulbous tip. The mouth and overall expression are highly mobile and elastic—a perfect vehicle for displaying the many emotions capable of this most universal of signs. One of Pisces classic representatives is the great Piscean mystic-scientist Albert Einstein.

The Type 1 Piscean prefers loose, casual dress, and everything seems to be either falling apart around them, or falling off them! Posture is notably poor, stoop shouldered or slouched, and hair is worn loose and untidy. As Pisces corresponds to the feet, their feet and footgear are notable in some way. In fact, both Piscean types seem to hate to have their feet enclosed. The voice is sad, weak or whiney, and usually of a higher tone.

MANNER *(For Type 1 Piscean)*

These Pisceans are rather slow, relaxed, resigned and negative in manner. However, they are capable of much sympathy, affection and charm. Neither pushy nor ambitious, they are of a gentle, easy-going and somewhat sloppy manner, disinclined toward any immediate action or goal. They are loving, elfin, sweet and affectionate. This is a psychically magnetic, dreamy and mediumistic type. Both Piscean types may appear tired, sleepy, quietly brooding or depressed. Realistically, the Manner described for Type 1 and Type 2 are interchangeable and good portrayals of both mood types could attend either Piscean physical type.

TYPE 2 PISCEAN

This second expression of Pisces brings to mind old illustrations of fairy-folk and elves. Facial features are small and pretty, with the petiteness of the Mercurian and all the sweetness of the Venusian. The nose is small and indefinite or upturned. The mouth is either fine-lipped or of the rose-bud type, with its expression quizzical or seductive. Mona Lisa smiles are typical of this type. Their lovely, large eyes (not bulging or too large as in Type 1) possess a characteristic elfin twinkle. Facial bones are weak, providing the face with a soft, rounded or oval form, and sweet dimples.

The complexion runs medium to fair in receptive populations, unlike the somewhat darker caste Type 1 Piscean. The body type is petite and slender, dainty and well-knit, much like the opposite sign, Virgo. Like the Virgo type, this Piscean type is tidily and tastefully attired. These Pisceans transport themselves with soundless grace. Both the great male ballet dancers, Nureyev and Nijinski, were born in this sign. The hands and feet of this type are dainty and well-formed.

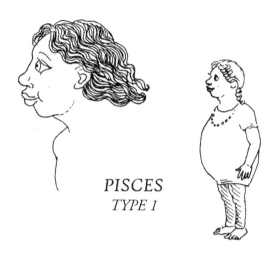

PISCES
TYPE 1

PISCES
TYPE 2

MANNER *(For Type 2 Piscean)*

The manner of the Type 2 Piscean is fairy-like, and they seem almost invisible. They will appear as if out of nowhere and disappear just as easily. Walking quietly and smoothly, they appear to float above the floor. Soft-spoken, elusive and shy, of an altogether gentle expression, women of this type fare better in this world than do the men. This is a notably passive and peaceful type. The mind works faster than in Type 1 Pisceans, showing all of Virgo's facility with detail combined with Piscean fluidity. Pisceans are either chatterboxes or talk so little as to bore others. This second type of Piscean is clever, almost Mercurial, and chameleon-like. They seem to fit in everywhere, quickly adopting the mannerisms and language of those around them—sometimes so much so that you wonder what the "real" personality is! Extreme pleasantness and charm are hallmarks.

PISCES TYPE 3

Seen mostly (but not exclusively) in males, this Piscean type is more reminiscent of fellow water sign Scorpio, though far more diffuse, poetic and delicate. The face is sad, the mood melancholic but good natured. These folks are deep. The eyes and general manner is profound, brooding, depressed. Sometimes their affect is flat, although when moved, the face is elastic and surprisingly expressive. (Nobody makes strange faces better than Pisces!) In negative types, the head hangs as if they have given up all hope, and have stopped trying to improve. They may shuffle along, stoop shouldered, hands hanging loose. Or conversely, if devoted to yoga, with great fluidity and perfect posture!

Dark eyes and hair are most common (in Caucasians), and the eyebrows are brooding but expressive. As in all Pisceans, there is not much facial structure. The facial features of this type are a bit

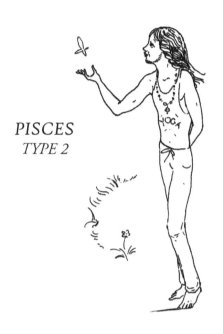

PISCES
TYPE 2

PISCES
TYPE 3

nondescript, although the overall look is "handsome," with those classically haunting, sensitive eyes.

The stature is short to medium and never strongly muscled, but more delicate: either thin or pudgy. Often, one senses a physical weakness or delicacy, as if the vital force is waning.

These are the natural poets, mystics and musicians. The atmosphere is negative and definitely depressive, yet soothing to those in mental suffering. Type 3 Pisceans are never too happy with this present earth plane, and dislike hard work. Look down—often the shoes worn out or missing entirely.

The voice is often fuzzy, tired or depressive, while simultaneously comforting, strangely beguiling or even hypnotic. This type possesses a high degree of sex magnetism and is rarely at loss for admirers, despite their lack of physical strength and eccentric ways. Type 3 natives are dependably generous and kind, but can morph into isolation, apathy and profound depressions. When in a bad mood, this type evinces more sarcasm and sometimes a mean streak not typical of the sign Pisces. These folks make gifted mystics.

PISCES TYPE CAREERS

All careers requiring personal sensitivity, sacrifice, solitude or diffused consciousness. Beware of excessive mental focus, positions of command or any work requiring personal ambition or aggression.

Nun, monk, psychic, photographer, solitary night worker, musician, poet, heir, minister, actor, lighting or sound specialist, intuitive (as opposed to graphic) artist, dancer, sound mixer, fish or footwear worker, hobo, charity worker, museum and library worker, circus and zookeeper, clown, child-care workers, fairy tale writer, novelist, sailor, surfer, holistic health practitioner (in combination with Scorpio, Capricorn or stronger signs), songwriter, renunciate, animal reserve worker, antique dealer, used clothing dealer, social service worker.

OVERVIEW

One in two Piscean people will evince traits of a classic Pisces appearance). Be sure to also check the Moon sign and the rising sign. Pisces is a hybrid of the Water Element, the Mutable Mode, the planets Jupiter and Neptune. All types exist, plus the three Pisces Decanate modifications *(see page 171)*.

PISCES TRADEMARKS

Remarkable footwear, open-toed shoes, peculiar feet, size extremes

PISCES SIGNATURES:

- sweet, dreamy, angelic and twinkling eyes
- very large eyes, sometimes protruding
- some types have deep, brooding eyes
- a very "giggly" sign, especially in females
- beautiful "Cupid's bow" mouth or full, loose-lipped, unrefined mouth
- flexible, expressive lips
- talks too much or too little
- tired, whining or depressed voice
- soft spoken
- extremely flexible, expressive face
- slightly rounded, slightly upturned nose
- weak chin, weak facial structure
- some types are stoop shouldered
- full hair (males tend to keep hair), rounded hairline
- tends toward shorter stature in the available gene pool
- body is either slender, delicate, amazingly flexible, fluidic, and extra-ordinarily graceful (reminding one of fairies) or; round, soft and phlegmatic in the extreme, carrying water weight
- manner is weak, sweet, tired, delicate, passive, depressed, easy going and cheery, affectionate
- magnetic appeal, sexy and affectionate
- huge appetites
- friendly, but can be shy
- shoe and foot eccentricities
- gentle, retiring manner
- chameleons
- extremely mobile and elastic facial expressions

THE PLANETARY TYPES

As Above

...So Below

The Ruler

SUN

RULES LEO

SOLAR THOUGHTS AND EMOTIONS

Positive: Willful, vital, commanding
confident, authoritative, positive, sunny, playful

Negative: Bossy, egocentric, vain, self-centered, hedonistic,
overly willful, proud

MANNER

Solar types are cheerful, bright, warm and regal. They are self-confident, commanding and self-possessed, although the type is also capable of flagrant displays of passionate emotion. Sometimes haughty and disdainful in manner, Sol's children are self-confident, and aware of their good looks and magnetism.

BODY PARTS

The Sun rules the heart and, through its sign Leo, bears some correspondence with the back. The right eye in the male and the left eye in the female are Sun-ruled.

BODY TYPE

The Apollonian or Solar type is of medium height with a shapely and graceful physique. The Solar type's description best matches that of the heroic statues of ancient Greece. True Solar types are rare. When near the Ascendant at birth, the Sun's position seems to physically emphasize the zodiac sign type of the Sun or even the Sun's opposite sign, (rather than the Solar type itself).

Solar types are harmoniously proportioned, possessing a strong and vital countenance. The chest is full and muscular. The shoulders are broad and the back and upper arm muscles

SUN

Sun or "Sol" is characterized by purpose and willpower

admirably developed. William G. Benham describes the Apollonian type in his classic, *The Laws of Scientific Hand Reading*. He also reports a "spring" in the walk and a long, full and muscular neck, altogether smooth and displaying neither Adam's apple nor muscle cords.

The teeth are finely formed. The body is naturally warm-blooded, similar to the Jupiterian. They have a Martian-Venusian-Leo body mix. This type gets thick in mid-life, unlike the lean Martian whom otherwise is quite similar. A remarkably handsome, well-made type.

HEAD AND FACE SHAPE

The Solar head is large, muscular and round or round-square, with a broad forehead of medium height. The face is broad, particular in the region of the eye and cheekbones. The traditionally Apollonian, or Solar type, bears much in common facially with the Venusian and Leonian.

FACIAL STRUCTURE

Solar cheeks are found and rosy, very firm, with no visible hollows. High cheekbones are typical.

EYES

The large eyes are almond-shaped and slant upwards in the feline manner. The eyes bear a self-contented, haughty gaze, yet sparkle with vitality and magnetism.

NOSE

The nose is straight, finely made, with characteristically Leonine flaring nostrils.

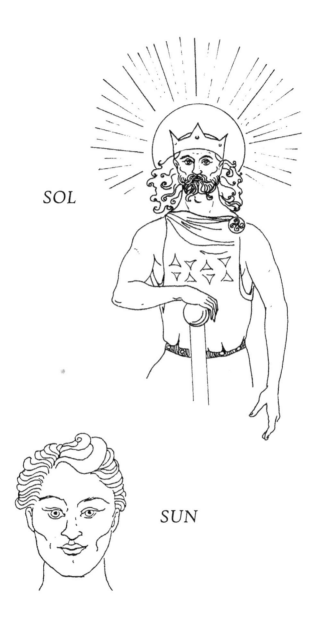

SOL

SUN

MOUTH

The mouth possesses a graceful outline, inclined to fullness with a curl or sneer to the upper lip in the manner of Elvis Presley.

VOICE

Sonorous and booming.

SKIN

The skin is flushed about the cheeks. In age, Solar types develop deep and sweeping folds of skin from nose flanges to the outer corner of the mouth, and jowls. Think of Alfred Hitchcock.

HAIR

The hair resembles a Sun-burst or lion's mane and may tend to red or blonde coloration (in Caucasian types).

HANDS

Expect to see a large, strong thumb, prominent first and fourth finger and a pink to red skin color (in Caucasian specimens). A healthy, well-formed hand.

DRESSING STYLE

Garish or flamboyant with a preference for bright warm colors. Gold is the Sun's color and gold his metal. Sol's traditional gem is the Ruby. Solar types love lots of loud jewelry, neck chains, capes and large pendants.

SOLAR TYPE CAREERS

Employer, manager, actor, goldsmith, theater owner, film director, producer.

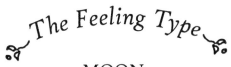

The Feeling Type

MOON
RULES CANCER

LUNAR THOUGHTS AND EMOTIONS

Positive: Sensitive, receptive, nurturing, tender, poetic, responsive, protective

Negative: Timid, submissive, short-sighted, reactive, hyper-sensitive, irrational, excessively subjective, smothering

MANNER

Gentle and sensitive. Lunarians who embody the Maternal archetype are motherly in every aspect: kindly, patient with others, quite talkative and extremely sociable. The aura is never intellectual, although higher types exude a beguiling poetic quality. Lunarians are an extremely responsive, emotional type. They are cautious until they feel safe and accepted, then they become trusting and friendly. However, much of th;s depends on the Moon's sign position because the Moon is so greatly colored by sign quality. Should Luna be prominent in the horoscope, a careful assessment must be made of the Moon's sign and the physical description of this sign. Sometimes the sign will predominate; at other times the pure Lunar type will predominate, regardless of sign.

BODY PARTS

Breasts, stomach, womb. Fertility. The left eye in the male and the right eye in the female.

BODY TYPE

Soft and round. The shoulders are distinctly narrow and sloping. Stomach and hips protrude. Overall body shape is round or teardrop. The arms are short and weak; the legs are thick and short. The flesh is very soft, and the body fat of a watery nature. Lunarians are inclined to water-bloat. The breasts are noticeable in some extreme (very large or very small).

HEAD AND FACE SHAPE

Distinctly round. The cue-ball type head. The head tends to be small. Facial bones appear non-existent. The face is quite flat and round and the forehead low and bulging, or narrow.

CHIN AND JAW

The Lunarian is decidedly weak-jawed, and receding chins are typical. May have no appreciable jaw development. The frontal chin and jaw outline continue the circle of the facial shape.

EYES

The Lunar eye is deep-set and protected. The upper lid is hardly visible. The eye is set very flat and forward looking in the head. Eyesight is weak. Eye color tends to pale, watery tones. Eyes are either very moist or very dry. Near-sightedness is common to the type. Eyes may slant downward at outer corners.

NOSE

The Lunarian nose is low, flat and formless, rarely demonstrating the full strong nose development of Martians, Saturnians or Jupiterians. Occasionally the nose is dainty, upturned and childlike.

MOUTH

There are two distinct types of mouth. The most common is the small slit mouth. These lips are fine to visibly non-existent. The best of the type reveals itself as a tiny "rosebud" mouth with a

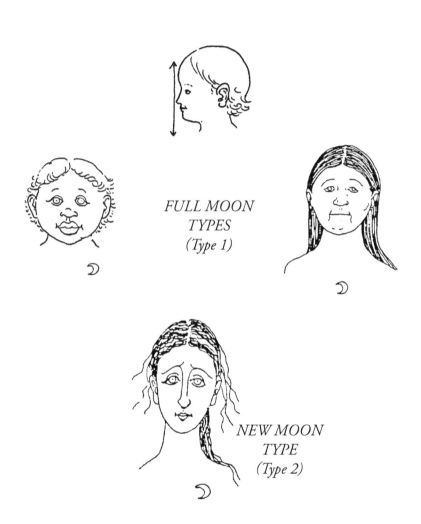

FULL MOON
TYPES
(Type 1)

NEW MOON
TYPE
(Type 2)

Lunar types are characterized by feeling and response.

sweet expression. The second Lunarian mouth type is large and loose-lipped, sometimes slack-jawed, and of poor definition.

VOICE

Meek and mild. The tone tends toward higher ranges and possesses little force.

SKIN

The skin is pale and very sensitive. Lunarians cannot endure the Sun's rays and are happier at night or on dark or foggy days.

HAIR

Lunarians possess a wide range of hair types. Very thick, lustrous, wavy hair is common. This type never balds. Equally common is the ultra-fine haired Lunarian. In some cases, the hairline grows extremely low. Hairline is rounded.

HANDS

Very small and smooth. The palm is round and the short, conically-shaped fingers are plump at the base. The outer percussion of the hand is raised high and full. Hands are cool and (in Caucasians) tend to be white, with translucent nails.

DRESSING STYLE

Lunarians prefer peasant dress. However, as this type is also conservative and enjoys conforming to tribal standards, the Lunarian typically selects attire conforming to the norm of the day. They also tend toward functional dress. They enjoy natural fibers and historic jewelry such as Celtic broaches or museum replica earrings. Aprons, shawls and scarves are typical as is warm, protective clothing. Being cool-bodied, the type is usually overdressed. Lunarians love pins, meaningful necklaces, pearls, and jewelry that reminds them of loved ones. The Lunar gems are pearl and moonstone. Silver is her traditional metal.

Lunarians are sentimentally attached to their clothing and will wear the same coat, bracelet or shoes over and over again. Being self-protective, Lunarians hide behind large coats, sunglasses, hair or too much clothing. They are often a sloppy type. The level of tastefulness depends a lot on the sign the Moon is in.

Note: The Lunar Type 1 and Type 2 Cancerians are quite different.

LUNAR TYPE CAREERS

Mother, cook, child-care worker, early childhood educator, small business operator, shop-keeper, tavern and coffee house owner, social worker, nurse, healer, homemaker, herbalist, psychic, poet, musician, singer, photographer, novelist, politician, actor

LUNAR MANNER

The Communicator

MERCURY

RULES VIRGO & GEMINI

MERCURIAL THOUGHTS AND EMOTIONS

Positive: Curious, clever, quick, logical, witty, skillful, discriminative

Negative: Cunning, crafty excessively intellectual, nervous, scattered, uncommitted, finicky

Mercurial thoughts produce fine, thin, pointy, quick and mobile shapes.

MANNER

Witty, talkative, quick, perky and alert. True Mercurians evade entanglements quickly. They have a very bright and cheerful manner, with a seeming excess of nervous energy that causes them to function at a faster pace than most other types. Passionate emotion are not apparent. They are flirtatious and mischievous. The facial expressions are extremely mobile and the type makes an excellent mimic or ventriloquist. The arms are always active, with the hands gesturing and talking. All motions are completed with ease as quick as the twinkling of an eye.

BODY PARTS

Nerves, hands, fingers, arms, speech, sense of hearing.

BODY TYPE

The body is petite and very agile. Being the quickest moving of the planetary types, Mercurians make excellent acrobats. The frame is slender and petite in Virgo and gracefully narrow and lanky in Gemini. This is a smooth and non-muscular type, although very wiry and flexible. Hips and shoulders are narrow.

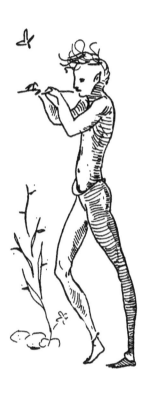

MERCURY

HEAD AND FACE SHAPE

Smallish, oval to oval-round head with high or bulging forehead, weak facial bones, and tapered chin.

CHIN AND JAW

The jaw is nondescript, while the chin, though small, is well-formed, pointed at the tip and long or upturned at the end.

EYES

Virgo Mercurians tend towards small, alert and inset eyes, whereas the Gemini Mercurians possesses large, wide open and twinkling eyes. They share a witty and mischievous expression. Eyebrows are fine and tend to point at the ends.

NOSE

The Mercurial nose is petite and fine, with small, clearly defined nostrils. The tip is often upturned slightly, with an elfin look. Ticks and twitches are not uncommon. Generally, the nose has a sharp, or even pinched look.

MOUTH

Mercurians have tiny or long, thin and precisely drawn mouths that are sharp, especially at the corners. Being a talkative type, the Mercurian has a mouth that is usually in motion and very expressive. The teeth are small, white and evenly set in pink gums.

VOICE

High and bright, or shrill or piercing.

HAIR

Mercurial hair is very fine and thin, and there is not much of it. The color is weak or drab, tending to be fair or mousy in shade. Beards and mustaches are kept exceptionally neat and trim and are often pointy at the tips or ends.

MERCURIAL MANNER

Mercury is characterized by wit, quickness and ease of motion.

SKIN

Mercurians have very fine, delicate and dry skin. This type rarely tans successfully, if at all.

HANDS

The hands are very prominent in the Mercury type, either skilled and useful in Virgo or expressive and quick in Gemini. The hands are small and smooth-fingered with pointed finger tips in Virgo and long and smooth-fingered in Gemini. The pinkie is long and pronounced in some way, e.g. bent, crooked, or set too high or low in the hand. The nails are trim and the hands kept well-groomed. This type gesticulates a lot with the hands when talking. Their hands are usually preoccupied.

WALK

Fast and agile, Mercurians are never loud or heavy on their feet. They are a very spry and youthful type.

DRESSING STYLE

(See "Virgo" and "Gemini.") Green emerald is Mercury's gem.

MERCURIAL TYPE CAREERS

Juggler, thief, writer, reporter, journalist, disc jockey, pool or card shark, magician, salesperson (with Mars), string and wind instrumentalist, crafts person, all communications careers, messenger, postman, travel agent, information expert, librarian, ventriloquist, puppeteer, cartographer (with Saturn), cartoonist, illustrator, taxi driver, porter, waiter, secretary, telephone operator.

The Harmonizer

VENUS

RULES TAURUS & LIBRA

VENUSIAN THOUGHTS AND EMOTIONS

Positive: Attractive, harmonious, loving, social, beautiful, cooperative, refined, diplomatic, graceful, charming, affectionate, concerned, artistic

Negative: Vain, indolent, lazy, shallow, self-satisfied, greedy, hedonistic, indecisive, weak, lacking direction

Venusian thoughts and feelings express themselves physically in oval, gracefully flowing lines.

MANNER

Venusians are poised and easy-going, altogether approachable and friendly. They are affectionate and warm-natured but never inappropriately demonstrative, intrusive or pushy. Venusians have a quieting and relaxing influence on those around them, and tend to cheerfulness. This is a happy, contented, pretty and sociable type with a relaxed and pleasant attitude.

BODY PARTS

Venus has some connection through Libra with the skin, and through Taurus with the vocal chords, the sound of the voice, and the ears, mouth and neck. Venus also has connections with the hair, veins, venous blood and female genitalia, ovaries, and thymus gland.

BODY TYPE

The Venusian stands medium to tall in height. The bodily contours are smooth and graceful with little muscular or bony prominence. The limbs are smooth and graceful, The weight ranges from willowy slenderness to plump, as the type is greatly addicted to sugar, although obesity is rare. Poise and balance are Venusian hallmarks.

SPECIAL MARKS

Dimple or cleft in chin, dimpled cheeks, "Cupid's bow" or rosebud mouth. Venusians of both genders ar beautiful.

HEAD AND FACE SHAPE

The Venusian head is smooth and oval. The facial bones are never prominent. The forehead is high, the cheeks low.

EYES

The eyes are large, heavy lidded and quite beautiful. The eyelashes are long and pretty. Venusian eyebrows are high and gracefully curved. Eyes are set apart with a "wide-open" expression.

EARS

Small and exquisitely formed.

NOSE

There are two distinct Venusian noses:

1. The Libran nose is dainty and refined, of small to medium size.
2. The Taurean nose is soft, sensual and inclines to be broad and spreading.

In either type, the nose is never pointy, harsh or aquiline.

MOUTH

The "Cupid's bow" mouth is the quintessential Venusian mouth. The Libra Venusian type possesses a sweet, serene mouth with soft, medium-sized, graceful lips. The upper lip is particularly

VENUS
TYPES

*The baby-face
Libra type.*

Venus is characterized by love, harmony and beauty.

beautiful in shape. The Taurean-Venusian types possess very full, heavy, sensual lips with the entire mouth inclining to be large and broad.

VOICE

Mellifluous voices in any range, Venusian voices are gentle, trusting and reassuring. Venusians make excellent orators and vocalists.

CHIN

Soft and gracefully rounded, may incline to be weak. Double chins easily acquired.

HAIR

Venusians possess soft-textured, finely waving and very lustrous, beautiful hair.

SKIN

Venusian skin is velvety to the touch, lovely and smooth. However, if Venus is seriously afflicted, the type can be prone to acne or other skin afflictions, a trait shared with Martians.

HANDS

Venusian hands are long, soft, well-padded and very warm to the touch. The hand may lack firmness in some types. The overall appearance is graceful and artistic. The fleshy pad at the base of the thumb is large and full. Fingertips range from long and tapered (Libra-Venusian) to square-tipped (Taurus-Venusian).

WALK

Graceful and poised, unhurried. Sometimes elegant or even stately if Saturn is strong.

DRESSING STYLE

VENUSIAN MANNER

The Venusian is tasteful and delights in good clothing and jewelry. They match their colors well, and are addicted to elegance. Venusian women like high-heeled shoes, pretty dresses, bows, frills and make-up, usually expertly applied. White, pinks and light blues are favorites. The men tend to effeminate and elegant tastes. Both sexes relish comfort, and therefore often go casual. Despite all of their elegance, Venusians can be surprisingly sloppy. It benefits true Venusians to wear diamonds. Copper is the metal of Venus.

VENUSIAN TYPE CAREERS

Artist, beautician, designer, cosmetician, model, receptionist, arbitrator, courtesan, singer, musician, cook, dancer (with Mars).

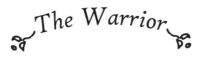 

The Warrior

MARS
RULES ARIES & SCORPIO

MARTIAN THOUGHTS AND EMOTIONS

Positive: Courageous, direct, forthright, ambitious, energetic, pioneering, inspired, purposeful, vigorous, passionate

Negative: Angry, combative, impatient, aggressive, intrusive, arrogant, selfish, lustful, cruel

Martian thoughts and feelings express themselves physically in angular, square, jutting, sharp and pointed shapes.

MANNER

Forthright and direct. This type is very alert and misses nothing. They seem "ready-to-spring" and physically confident. The manner is always intense and active. Negative Martians can be irreverent, rude and saucy. Their gestures are angular and their mannerisms of the masculine variety. They are completely capable of socially unacceptable behavior, such as putting their shoes on your table or spitting on the sidewalk. The best types possess absolute courage, valor and fantastic vitality.

BODY PARTS

Mars seems to have some association (through its sign Aries) with the head, left ear, eyes and hair. It is also associated with red blood corpuscles, the adrenal glands, testosterone, and male genitalia.

BODY TYPE

Martians are usually of medium height with short, muscular legs. The body is muscular, lithe and lean. This is a decidedly athletic type. Martian types walk proudly with their shoulders erect. The

MARS MANNER

Mars is characterized by energy, courage and the warrior spirit.

type is youthful, graceful and well-formed in every way, and is highly prone to physical pride and vanity.

SPECIAL MARKS

Widow's peak or "V" hairline, red hair, moles, scars, acne.

HEAD AND FACE SHAPE

The Martian head type is square and angular, with a well accented jaw line and cheekbones. Sometimes there is a strong development at the base of the skull, above the neck. Two types of foreheads are common. The first is very low, with a low hairline, often sloped backwards. The second type is high and straight, balancing the strong nose and chin, giving the look of a proud and lordly warrior. When viewed in profile, the back crown of the head may rise higher than the front.

EYES

The eye is medium to large. The gaze is extremely penetrating and there is a "fire" in the eye. Brows are low, well developed and may overhang. Eyebrows are heavy and of a wiry texture, sometimes joining across the nose bridge. Martian eyes will be noticed! The eye color is very intense.

EARS

The ears are either small and set close to the head, or jutting out and forward. They incline to red or purple coloration and may be pointy looking.

NOSE

The Martian nose comes in two types. The eagle or hawk nose has a firm tip, strong bridge and often a sharp contour. Nostrils are sharp and sometimes flaring. The second nose type is the blunted boxer's nose, with a squarish, pugged, bulldog look.

MOUTH

The Martian mouth is firm, and comes in many sizes. Sometimes the lips are harshly outlined, or pulled tight. The lines running at the sides of the mouth are strongly cut, the lips quite red.

CHIN AND JAW

Martians have square or pointed chins and are very angular about the jaw. "Lantern" jaws are not uncommon. In the best specimens, the jaw flange can be seen from the back of the head. The chin is strong and long, balancing the powerful, aquiline nose. In very aggressive Martians, the lower jaw juts forward, giving the appearance of an under-bite.

VOICE

The Martian voice is youthful, harsh and loud.

SKIN

Martian skin is reddish, rough and thick. Pits, gashes, scars and moles are common marks of Mars. Martians are acne prone.

HAIR

The hair is course and wiry. Often tightly curled or intensely colored, the hair will stand out in some manner. Red hair is common. The beard is short, harsh and very thick, inclining to reddish tints. A pointed, *widow's peak* hairline is a classic mark of Mars.

HANDS

The Mars hand is remarkably square, hard and red. Lines of the hand are few and deeply cut. The mid and center palm is raised. The lower palm is well developed. Fingers are square or spatulate at the tips.

 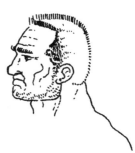

MARS
TYPES

DRESSING STYLE

The Martian is athletically body-conscious and can be every bit as vain as the Venusian or Solar types. They love fitted clothing that reveals their fine musculature and are never modest. Male Martians love Western wear, short sleeves, or a machismo look in any fashion style. The women dress in a flashy, revealing manner and enjoy attracting attention. Both sexes seem to love colors of the red family. Tattoos were made for the Martian type. The stone of Mars is red coral and his metal is iron. Most red stones, including bloodstones, ruby and garnet have some association with Mars.

MARTIAN TYPE CAREERS

Athlete, soldier, mechanic, surgeon, explorer, fire-fighter, police officer, locksmith, attorney, physical educator, stunt-person, blacksmith, carpenter, engineer, tool-maker, foundry and metal worker, dancer (with Venus), sculptor (with Saturn), butcher, exterminator, lifeguard, construction worker.

The Benefactor

JUPITER
RULES SAGITTARIUS & PISCES

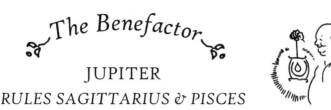

JUPITARIAN THOUGHTS AND EMOTIONS

Positive: Joyous, hopeful, faithful, generous, carefree, noble, inclusive, tolerant, broad-minded, enthusiastic, open

Negative: Boastful, bombastic, overconfident, careless, extravagant, egotistic, foolhardy

Jupiter's thoughts and feelings express themselves physically as large, voluminous, oblong or founded shapes, whirlwinds, and expansive gestures and motions.

MANNER

The Jupiterian is remarkable in that he appears at once lordly and grand yet cheerful and friendly. Jupiterian gestures are expansive, majestic and full. Jupiterians uplift, hearten and enthuse those around them without apparent need to receive such stimulus from others to keep themselves happy.

BODY PARTS

Jupiter rules the liver and fat production, and insulin production in the pancreas (the Islets of Langerhans). Through its sign Sagittarius, Jupiter has some correspondence with the arteries and arterial circulation.

BODY TYPE

Jupiterians are large. They are of medium height but stoutly and strongly built. Their ample flesh is solid rather than watery or spongy. The frame is built to carry heavy weight. The body, though heavy or obese, is carried with a stately grandeur. Some types are rectangular in build, squared from shoulder to hip with medium to long legs. This type generally carries much solid weight and resembles a football blocker. Jupiterians are exceptionally warm-blooded and will startle others by wearing T-shirts in bitter weather. They produce their own heat well, perspiring freely. Back, chest, shoulders and upper arms are broad and thick, predominating over the hips and legs. The appearance of both sexes is tank-like.

SPECIAL MARKS

The mark of Jupiter is a single strong vertical line between the brows—one indication of a philosophical disposition. Jupiterians often have a "clown's tip" or bulbous development at the tip of the nose.

HEAD AND FACE SHAPE

Look for the distinctly large and beautifully domed head of oblong contour. The top of the head is full and rounded—never flat or square. The face is oblong in shape, i.e. an elongated circle.

FACIAL STRUCTURE

Full cheeks and jowls predominate over bone structure (which, although always substantial, is not a significant fact of facial appearance). A delicate, noble cheekbone is high but non-protruding and there is rarely any evidence of cheek hollows. The face is fleshy and pink.

CHIN AND JAW

The Jupiterian has a large, well formed chin—perhaps the largest of all types. The tip is either rounded or a little squared. Double and triple chins jowls, and flowing Santa Claus beards are all common Jupiterian trademarks. The jaw is strong, firm, although not excessively so, and fleshy. Some Jupiterians display a dimple at the tip of the chin. The cheeks are pink and "cheeky."

JUPITER

Jupiter is characterized by joy and beneficence.

EYES

There are two types of Jupiterian eyes. The classic noble eye seen in portraits of great statesmen exemplifies one type of Jupiterian eye. This eye type is moderate to large with a mild, tolerant, brave and honorable expression. The lids are full and exposed. Eyebrows are high and either arched or expanded upwards at the end. The brow bones are high and well formed although never excessively so as in the Martian type.

The second Jupiterian eye type is small and possess a merry twinkle; think of Santa Claus eyes. This second eye type will accompany an overall Santa Claus appearance, to perfection: cherry nose, pink cheeks, obese, etc.

MOUTH

The Jupiterian mouth is full, broad, and firm in the best types. The upper lip may be prominent. The two front teeth may be noticeable.

VOICE

The voice is positively booming. The characteristic Jupiterian laugh is loud, resonant and strong. Baritones and basses are common for Jupiterian men. Voice tone is cheerful and confident.

SKIN

Jupiterians have smooth, clear and pink skin. The skin may incline to red if the Jupiterian malady of high-blood pressure is present.

HAIR

Jupiterians are very extreme in regard to hair. They either possess very thick, dense hair or none at all. Male Jupiterians are famous for their classic bald domes of high and perfect proportions. However, the hairy Jupiterian will never bald, retaining the

JUPITER MANNER

hairline of boyhood well into middle age. The beard is very full and flowing in the more bohemian types, producing a grand and patriarchal appearance.

HANDS

The hand is extremely large and full-fleshed (as are the feet). The first-finger (the pointer) is long and strong, and in pure Jupiterians, observation will reveal the other three fingers of the hand leaning strongly towards it.

DRESSING STYLE

The Jupiterian prefers full, loose, robe-like garments. Women incline to pile their hair dome-like on their heads. Jupiterians love sandals and non-restrictive footwear, possibly due to their tendency to overheat. They love color, especially turquoise blue, although they are rarely garish. Jupiter's gemstone is yellow sapphire or yellow topaz. The metal of Jupiter is tin.

JUPITARIAN TYPE CAREERS

Teacher (especially higher education), loan agent, clown, actor, politician, general, priest, bishop, philanthropist, publisher, advertiser, financier, clergyman, astrologer, guru, worker for social change.

The Maker of Order

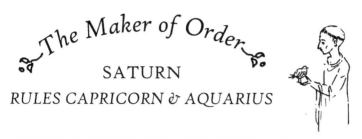

SATURN

RULES CAPRICORN & AQUARIUS

SATURNIAN THOUGHTS AND FEELINGS

Positive: Circumspect, wise, practical, deep, logical, prudent, frugal, disciplined, responsible

Negative: Melancholic, fearful, inhibited, stingy, loveless, cold, depressed, dense, critical, bureaucratic, inflexible, faithless, unsympathetic

MANNER

Saturnians are reserved, cool and dignified. They are also introverted and self-respecting. They do not inspire others to spontaneously run up and hug them. The best types have beautiful, erect posture and carry themselves with the simple dignity of great yogis. Their air is solemn and pensive. The vibration is slow, deep and inspires seriousness in others, never mirth. Deep sincerity and contemplativeness are obvious in the manner of higher type Saturnians. The atmosphere of the lower type Saturnian is negative, misanthropic, and dejected. Think of Scrooge in *A Christmas Carol.*

BODY PARTS

Saturn has some rulership over the bones, cartilage, ligaments, teeth, sense of hearing, the right ear, and the skin and nails. The gall bladder has some association with Saturn.

BODY TYPE

Saturnians are cold, stiff and prone to rheumatism or other arthritic complaints. The body is narrow throughout, with protruding shoulder blades, ribs and knees. Various joints and knobs of the bony structure are large and protruding. Shoulders are narrow, bony and held high and stiff. This is the classic ectomorph.

HEAD AND FACE SHAPE

The Saturnian head is long, narrow and medium to small in size. Facial angles and bony protrusions are well-defined. The forehead is high and narrow. A favorably placed Saturn in the birth chart may express an exceptional beauty of chiseled type.

EARS

Saturnian ears are large, very narrow and long-lobed. The ear is positioned close against the head.

NOSE

Saturnian noses are long and narrow. The skin of the nose is pulled tight, clearly revealing the bones at the bridge. Nasal angle is either straight or down-turned with its tip curving back toward the mouth. Nostrils are clearly defined.

MOUTH

The Saturnian mouth is a pale, tight slit. In extreme types the lips are non-apparent. Hairlines around the lips are common. Saturnian teeth are large and frequently in poor condition—chipped, yellow, brown, or misshapen. The gums may be unhealthy and receding.

CHIN AND JAW

The Saturnian jaw is both narrow and angular with a strong, squared or pointed chin. Jaw line, neck cords and Adam's apple are quite visible in both sexes.

VOICE

Saturn's voice is slow, deliberate and tending toward lower tones. This is a decidedly laconic type.

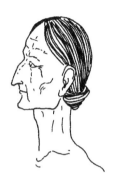 

SATURN

SATURNIAN MANNER

HAIR

Saturnian's have poor hair, skin, nails and teeth. The hair is dry, straight and prone to premature graying and dandruff problems (although not inclined to baldness). Hair luster is utterly lacking.

SKIN

Saturnian skin is very dry and flaky. In Caucasians, the complexion tends to be either yellowish or very pale and white. The skin either hangs in folds or is tightly drawn over the highly visible bone structure. Saturnian skin lines deep and heavily, adding to the overall appearance of respectable age and wisdom. Saturnians are extremely prone to eczema, moles and other skin disturbances.

HANDS

The Saturnian has exceptionally long, bony hands with notice-able knuckles and finger joints. Saturnian fingers are square-tipped, and as a rule have bad nails. Fingers are held closely together, thumb to hand. The middle finger is strong and dominant.

WALK

Higher types deport themselves gracefully and with dignity. The posture is poised and erect. In poor types, the posture is stooped as if beaten down by the woes of the world.

DRESSING STYLE

Conservative and simple. Higher Saturnian types prefer an attire both elegant and tasteful and can wear a suit better than anyone. Work clothes and overalls are equally common. This is an orderly type, inclined to simplicity and neatness. They prefer no jewelry, wear sensible shoes and dislike anything ostentatious. Saturnians prefer dark blues, blacks, grays, browns and beiges. Lapis Lazuli and blue sapphire are beneficial stones for true Saturnians.

SATURNIAN TYPE CAREERS

Architect, stonemason, scholar, curator, doctor, scientist, bureaucrat, administrator, government worker, builder, businessman, corporation head, farmer, bricklayer, judge, nun, monk, graphic artist, printer (with Mercury), leather worker, potter, real estate agent, land developer, gardener, grain dealer, plumber, night worker.

THE OUTER PLANETS
URANUS, NEPTUNE & PLUTO

When Neptune, Uranus or Pluto are prominent at birth, they express themselves more through the eyes and vibrational atmosphere of individuals than through physical characteristics. Due to their relatively recent discovery, Uranian, Neptunian and Plutonian physical types are still being observed and researched by modern astrologers. Since its discovery in 1930, Pluto hasn't completed one revolution of its orbit, so we remain ignorant of the full variations of the Plutonian physical type. For this reason the physical descriptions given for these three outer planetary types are generalized and less detailed than those provided for the Ptolemaic planets.

The Individualist
URANUS
CO-RULES AQUARIUS

URANIAN THOUGHTS AND EMOTIONS

Positive: Inventive, scientific, unique, inspired, genius, liberating, individual, electric, enervating

Negative: Shocking, bizarre, abrupt, radical, autocratic, extreme, spasmodic, irreverent

EXPRESSES AS...

A decidedly electrical feeling pervades the aura of a Uranian individual. Uranians possess a highly-charged mental atmosphere, and sometimes make less electrically charged types feel uneasy. Usually they are brilliant.

PHYSICAL EXPRESSION

Uranians are often extraordinarily tall. The upper head and forehead are very large, and the cool, light eyes are set quite far apart and possess a peculiarly electric, intelligent, yet cooly impersonal gaze. Egg-shaped heads are common. The Uranian trademark hair is very fair, thin and frizzy or wavy and completely impossible to manage. This tends to be among the blondest of types in receptive populations. The eyes can be sparkling blue. Facial features tend to be refined but otherwise unremarkable. The skin is very fair (in Caucasians).

There is normally something weird, disturbing, bizarre or extreme about the Uranian person. Mismatched or very oddly thrown-together outfits in bright colors are typical. Speech is rapid, full of multi-syllable words with peculiar observations and

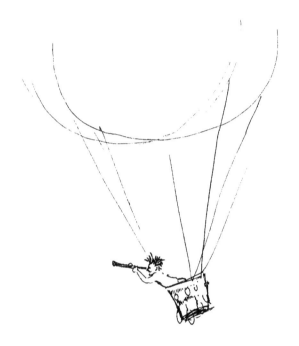

URANIAN MANNER

comments. Vocal tone may not be pleasant—some types have a computer-like quality to their voice. The body temperature is cool. People either love or loathe the Uranian—they are extremists and produce extreme reactions in others.

URANIAN TYPE CAREERS

Inventor, scientist, cartoonist, astrologer, aviator, balloonist, social commentator, odd-ball professional, revolutionary, computer specialist.

The Magnetic Mystic
NEPTUNE
CO-RULES PISCES

NEPTUNIAN THOUGHTS AND EMOTIONS

Positive: Mystical, poetic, compassionate, sympathetic, psychic, selfless, devotional

Negative: Listless, weak, indecisive, dependent, unrealistic, indiscriminate, addictive, deceptive, illusionary

EXPRESSES AS...

The Neptunian has a mysterious, elusive and extremely magnetic aura. Neptunians are seductive. They possess a vague and imprecise manner and generally seem tired and sad. They can be very beguiling and enigmatic. Vitality is low and this type may appear listless or depressed.

PHYSICAL EXPRESSION

Neptunians possess large, heavy-lidded eyes with an other-worldly expression. Some Neptunians look full of the world's sadness, their eyes all but brimming over with compassion. Other Neptunians possess angelic, sparkling eyes. Large facial features are quite common, and typically the features are ill-defined. The nose may appear heavy or lumpy. Lips may seem too large with poor outline. Facial bones are generally weak and the face inclines to be narrow. The voice is both very sweet and very tired.

Neptunians dress seductively and prefer loose or flowing garments. Things seem to be falling apart about them. Their aura is both soothing and draining to others. The type tends to be soft and non-muscular and can, in extreme cases, be prone to obesity of a watery nature. Typical Neptunians are of average height. Evolved Neptunians are truly angelic.

NEPTUNIAN TYPE CAREERS

Photographer, sailer, musician, poet, psychic, chemist, bartender, drug dealer, smuggler, con artist (with Mercury), distiller, oil worker, renunciate, advertiser, actor, writer (of fairy tales, mysteries, romance novels), psychologist (with Mercury), para-psychologist, oceanographer.

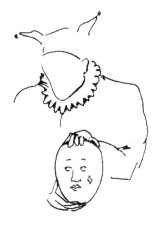

NEPTUNIAN MANNER

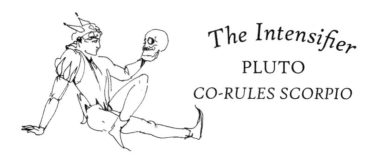

The Intensifier
PLUTO
CO-RULES SCORPIO

PLUTONIAN THOUGHTS AND EMOTIONS

Positive: Penetrating, analytical, powerful, surgical, resourceful, confident, managerial

Negative: Manipulative, murderous, cynical, destructive, sardonic, cruel, domineering, emotional extremes

EXPRESSES AS...

Plutonians are intense and brooding. Their atmosphere is of a great and potentially dangerous power held in reserve.

PHYSICAL EXPRESSION

Plutonians have extremely dark and penetrating eyes that seem to look through you and down into your soul. Dramatically overhanging brows shadow deep-set prominent eyes. The nose is eagle-like, or very pronounced. Plutonians are usually thickset swarthy, strong and hirsute. The Plutonian type replicates the Scorpio types exactly. A steely intensity of the eye is common to all persons with Pluto prominent at birth, but not necessarily the complete Scorpio appearance.

PLUTONIAN TYPE CAREERS

Detective, investigator, narcotics agent, excavator, archeologist, exterminator, mortician, forensics, epidemiology, Egyptologist, research scientist, refrigeration or nuclear power worker.

PLUTONIAN MANNER

SUMMARY
THE INTERRELATION OF THOUGHTS, FEELINGS & PHYSICAL FORMS

This study of planetary and sign types reveals how closely physical form conforms to thought. Generous thoughts produce broad features; critical thoughts express themselves as sharp or pointed features. Joy gladdens the expression, whereas fear sallows the face. Soft and gentle minds produce soft and gentle faces, just as aggressive thoughts create angular, projecting features.

True inner beauty is never hidden by uncomely features, and the reverse is also true, explaining why some of the world's great beauties are not so lovely to those who look closely. Beautiful thoughts and feelings create a beauty of expression if not of form, calling to mind those "homely" ones who have stirred our hearts to inwardly declare, "Now that is a beautiful face!"

Each of us must take responsibility for the face we project to others. The architect lives within, not without. We depart our study of Astrophysiognomy with the signature quote of the great psychic Edgar Cayce, who reminds us that *Mind is the Builder.*

THE LUNAR NODES
& PHYSICAL APPEARANCE

The effect of the South and North Lunar Nodes is primarily felt as a vibrational atmosphere around an individual. However, the nodes do have some impact on physical appearance when positioned within thirty degrees of the Ascendant at birth. This impact is strongest when a Node is located in the same sign as the Ascendant, and increases with proximity to the Ascendant degree. Extremes of stature such as dwarfism or extreme shortness or great height can occur if either node tenants this region. The South Node is more often associated with shortness and the North Node with tallness, although the reverse can also occur.*

Bruises, blemishes and a tendency for skin irritation and disease is typical of either node close to the Ascendant. Traditionally, both nodes have some association with mental illness, depression or neurological complaints. The South Node is more often coincident with a delicate constitution, low vitality and a weak immune system. Strength, endurance and vitality more often accompany the North Node. The color red is associated with the South Node; black is the North Node's traditional color.

The effect of the Lunar Nodes is very powerful upon the psychic nature. Their presence near the Ascendant must never be ignored. A sweet and retiring nature is typical for the South Node in this region. Such natives incline to spirituality, introversion,

* *Astrologer George White did some interesting research correlating Lunar Node position at birth with human stature, and may have been the first Westerner to report upon this phenomenon.*

acute sensitivity and lack of confidence. They may appear tired, weak or depressed. Their character is kindly, receptive and non-materialistic. The North Node produces intensity, excitability, and great ambition. Persons born with a prominent North Node should avoid becoming egocentric or fanatical. Their personalities are strong, willful and eccentric. North Node types are also powerful, mysterious and secretive.

Either node near the Ascendant (or conjoined the planetary ruler of the Ascendant), can indicate some great insecurity, complex or exceptional quality related to the bodily appearance. Many people born with the nodes so placed have been obsessively unhappy with their stature, name, gender or race. The sign the offending node is in can give clues to the source of the difficulty.

The "Dragon's Head" and the "Dragon's Tail,"
i.e. the Lunar Nodes, are always opposite each other.

PHYSICAL APPEARANCE RELATING TO PLANETARY CONJUNCTIONS WITH THE LUNAR NODES

Close planetary conjunctions (0–3 degrees orb) with the Lunar Nodes may reflect on the physical appearance. However it is good practice to find a second or third testimony in the chart before ascribing the traits listed below.

*North Node/**Sun:*** Great confidence, strength and vitality. Large head and torso. Big ego. Strongest effects for Leo Ascendant or if occurring in Fire signs. "The bully" if negative.

*South Node/**Sun:*** Low confidence, weak-willed. Inferiority complex (may outlet as excessive bravado). "The weakling" if negative. This is most apparent for Leo Ascendant or if South Node occurs in Libra or Aquarius.

*North Node/**Moon:*** Large breasts and stomach. Good appetite. Fertile. Prone to water retention and tumors. Popular. Strongest effects for Cancer Ascendant, or Moon in Cancer or Taurus.

*South Node/**Moon:*** Thin or frail body. Sensitive skin. Prone to extreme emotional sensitivity, allergies, depression, menstrual and uterine complaints, infertility, miscarriage, eating disorders, malnutrition. Strongest for Cancer Ascendant or if South Node is placed in Capricorn.

*North Node/**Mercury:*** Great gift with words and adept with fingers. Good writer. Strongest for Gemini and Virgo Ascendants, or if North Node is in Gemini, Virgo or Aquarius.

*South Node/**Mercury***: Neurological dysfunction, paralysis, stuttering, retardation, speech or hearing impairment. This is most pronounced for Gemini and Virgo Ascendants, or if South Node occurs in Gemini, Virgo, Sagittarius, or Pisces.

*North Node/**Venus***: Great Physical beauty, musical voice, lovely hair. This conjunction is strongest for Libra and Taurus Ascendants or if North Node occurs in Libra, Taurus, Gemini, Leo or Pisces.

*South Node/**Venus***: Poor hair or bad skin. Face is unremarkable, pocked or blemished. Likely to have a complex about one's beauty or attractiveness. Strongest in Virgo, Scorpio, Aries.

*North Node/**Mars***: Great physical strength and athletic prowess. Energy, vitality, command. Strong nose. Strongest effects for Aries or Scorpio Ascendants, or if North Node occurs in Fire signs (Aries, Leo, Sagittarius) or Scorpio.

*South Node/**Mars***: Either a lack of martial abilities or unpleasantly aggressive (especially in Aries and Scorpio). Scars and injuries to eyes and nose. Indicates a weak vitality, anemia or timidity if South Node occurs in Cancer. Accident prone in Aries.

*North Node/**Jupiter***: This is one testimony of a very large, tall or fat body and a jolly temperament. Tendency for fatty growths, water retention, diabetes and tumors. Lush hair and beards. Strongest for Sagittarius and Pisces Ascendants, or if North Node occurs in Sagittarius, Pisces or Cancer.

*South Node/**Jupiter***: Too little fat. The growth principle is disturbed. Most pronounced for Sagittarius and Pisces Ascendants, or if the South Node occurs in Capricorn. Diabetic tendency.

*North Node/**Saturn***: Strong bones and teeth. Longevity. Tendency to boney growths and arthritic complaints. Strongest for Capricorn and Aquarius rising or if North Node occurs in Capricorn, Aquarius or Libra.

*South Node/**Saturn***: Poor bones and bad teeth or hearing. The skin is heavily lined. Short stature. Prone to osteoporosis, rickets, tooth decay, and stooped posture. Strongest for Capricorn and Aquarius Ascendants or if South Node occurs in Cancer.

KARMA
& PHYSICAL ANOMALY

People who suffer from facial or bodily imperfections need not necessarily feel that these features describe their moral character, past or present. Beauty can be a curse; disability can encourage depth, courage and intelligence. True beauty is a quality that shines out from the inner being and is not dependent on the perfection of outer form. Whatever the source of our imperfections, it is wise to remember that in the grand scale of time and eternal life, these are never permanent.

Gross physical deformities, while seeming to result from various pre-natal or post-natal causes, may actually stem back to deeper karmic origins. Karma is meant to refer to previous life causes, i.e. the law of cause and effect operating from one life to another. There are several types of karma potentially involved in physical abnormalities. Four types of physical karma are documented below. Of course, physical karma works just as well in cases of extraordinary beauty or ability.

REPEAT OR MEMORY IMPRINT KARMA

An individual who dies from a violently produced wound is likely to be strongly imprinted by this trauma and may begin a new life with a similar wound or mark. Birthmarks, as well as physical handicaps, can result from karma of this type.

MISUSE KARMA

The misuse of any physical organ may result in either the weakening or malformation of that organ in a future life.

An example of misuse karma might be a previous life of freely indulged profanity resulting in a present life malformation of the mouth. Such an imprint can even be witnessed occurring within one lifetime! Disharmonious thoughts and actions create an unpleasant appearance in the corresponding organ. It is, however, encouraging to remember that the disharmonious thought forces behind physical malformations can be corrected through our positive efforts.

RECIPROCAL KARMA

This might be best thought of as eye-for-an-eye and tooth-for-a-tooth karma. As well as being the result of Memory Imprint or Misuse Karma, deformed or even missing limbs or features may reflect what we did to another in a previous incarnation. It is good to remember that such deeds were commonplace in ancient times, and in all probability we have each committed abominable deeds in the past. Such awareness will keep us from looking down our noses at those suffering from a possible Reciprocal Karma.

FAMILY KARMA

Some religions assert that the deformity of a child could be a form of atonement or working-out of the Reciprocal Karma or Misuse Karma of its parents or family group. Perhaps we take on deformities at sacrifice and service to our families or ancestors.

EXAMPLE PERSONALITIES

There are always drawbacks in presenting lists of living people. First, it is too easy to limit one's perception of sign or planetary types to one specific example. Secondly, skeptics will conclude that individual examples in each category fail to exactly resemble each other and are therefore arbitrary. Therefore, the reader is highly advised to digest the sign and planetary archetypes before reading these lists of famous examples.

Also, please bear in mind the endless variation which archetypes display at the individual level. Some examples, such as Burl Ives and Peter Ustinov, are found in two or more categories. This is because they strongly represent both categories and because certain planetary and sign archetypes bear much in common.

TWO USEFUL RULES FOLLOW:

1. A good example of a sign type **need not be actually born in the sign**. *[Refer to pages 33-34, Table of Physical Significators in the Birth Chart.]*

2. No two people can ever exactly resemble one another. Each person on the list is an **individual expression** of one or more sign or planetary types. *Example:* Abraham Lincoln and J. Krishnamurti look very different and yet both are extremely fine examples of the Saturnian type.

SIGNS

ARIES

TYPE 1: Lady Gaga, Jerry Brown, Helen Reddy (Mars rising in Aries), Mickey Rooney, Charleton Heston in his famous portrayal of Moses in *The Ten Commandments*, Patrick Swayze, Ted Dansen as the character Sam Malone in *Cheers*, Chuck Connors.

TYPE 2: Diana Ross, Pearl Bailey as a young woman, Frieda Kahlo, Chuck Connors.

TAURUS

Joe Louis, Burl Ives (Moon in Taurus), Peter Ustinov (Aries-Taurus cusp), Theodore Bikel, Fats Waller, Mae West (Leo with Taurus Ascendant; here we have the Leo face and the Taurus body), Honore De Balzac, Gerald Ford.

GEMINI

TYPE 1: Judy Garland, Peter Pan, Marilyn Monroe, Joel Gray in *Cabaret.*

TYPE 2: Bob Dylan, Art Garfunkel (Moon in Gemini), Pete Seeger (Moon in Gemini), George Bush, Jaques Yves Cousteau.

CANCER

TYPE 1–Full Moon Type: Charles Laughton, Burl Ives and Mikhail Gorbachov (each with Cancer Ascendant), Louis Armstrong, Julian Assange (Cancer Sun, Moon rising), Wally in *My Dinner With Andre*, Babe Ruth.

TYPE 2–New Moon Type: Mona Lisa, Joan Baez as a young woman (opposite Sun sign, Capricorn), Franz Kafka, Natalie Wood in *West Side Story*, Sal Mineo, PeeWee Herman when in his sad affect, Princess Diana.

LEO

Mama Cass Elliott, Mae West, Bill Clinton (Leo with Taurus Moon), Madonna, Lucille Ball, Jackqueline Onassis, Arnold Schwartznegger, Mick Jagger, Alabama ex-governor George Wallace (Leo-Virgo cusp, Moon, Mars, Jupiter, Mercury and Neptune in Leo), Zsa Zsa Gabor (opposite Sun sign Aquarius), Leontyn Price, Debbie Harry.

VIRGO

Michael Jackson (Virgo with a strong Pisces Moon), Greta Garbo, Shirley MacLaine and Patty Duke as young women, Michael J. Fox, Geraldine Ferraro, Fred McMurray, Hank Williams Sr. A quintessential example is Audrey Meadows as Alice in *The Honeymooners*.

LIBRA

Julie Andrews (a perfect example in *The Sound of Music*), Linda Darnell, Barbara K. Roberts, Fred Astaire (although not born in Libra, a strongly Venusian birth chart), Oscar Wilde, Montgomery Clift, Eleanore Roosevelt, Sidney Poitier (Moon, Saturn in Libra), Dwight D. Eisenhower, Jimmy Carter (baby-faced type).

OWL TYPE: John Lennon, Henry Kissinger (Moon, Saturn in Libra), Mahatma Gandhi.

SCORPIO

TYPE 1: Indira Gandhi, Grace Slick (combined with Mercurial qualities), Bonnie Raitt, Uri Geller (Moon, Jupiter, Venus in Scorpio and Ascendant at the Libra-Scorpio cusp), Cher (opposite Sun sign, Taurus) Sinéad O'connor, Morticia in the original *Addams Family* series.

TYPE 2: John Belushi in dark glasses, Michael Dukakis, Pablo Picasso, Al Capone.

SAGITTARIUS

TYPE 1: Andre in *My Dinner with Andre* (one could not find a more perfect example), Duke Ellington, Frank Sinatra as a young man, Jimi Hendrix, Bob Dylan (Sagittarius Ascendant), Sammy Davis Jr. (ideal face and expression although his body type is more indicative of his Virgo Moon), Arsenio Hall (ideal Sagittarian type), the character Sam Malone in *Cheers*.

TYPE 2: Ben Franklin, Santa Claus.

CAPRICORN

TYPE 1: Michelle Obama, David Bowie, Barbara Stanwick, Rod Serling, Joan Baez (combined with Venusian), Marlene Dietrich.

TYPE 2: Muhammad Ali, Oliver Hardy, Joe Frazier, Norman Schwarzkopf.

TYPE 3: Anthony Hopkins, Christopher Reeves as Superman/Clark Kent.

AQUARIUS

In voice and manner, Oprah Winfrey. Diane Keaton (Moon in Aquarius), Jim Neighbors (Moon in Aquarius), Julia Child (opposite Sun sign–Leo) exemplifies the bell-like voice, height, mannerism and character; Jimmy Stuart in *It's a Wonderful Life*, is quintessentially Aquarian. Aquarius and Capricorn are fellow Saturn-ruled signs, but Aquarius lends the look an eccentric twist.

"MERCURIAL" AQUARIAN: Charles Lindbergh, Ronald Reagan as a young actor, Cary Grant.

"VENUSIAN" AQUARIAN: Goldie Hawn, Jimmy Stewart in *It's a Wonderful Life*, Ellen DeGeneres.

"SATURNIAN" AQUARIAN: Paula Poundstone is a fine female example of the Saturnian Aquarian; Barack Obama, the male example, has Saturn rising in Aquarius. Abraham Lincoln, the

mature Virginia Woolf, Evangeline Adams, Vita Sackville-West (with Venus and Cancer New Moon), Ellen DeGeneres (with Venus).

PISCES

Johnny Cash, Ralph Nader, Curt Cobain and George Harrison are all good examples of the deep flowing, poetically somber type of Pisces so often encountered. This could be due to the influence of the Scorpio Decanate of Pisces *[See Table 4, page 171]*.

TYPE 1: Michael Jackson (Pisces Moon, Neptune rising), Edgar Cayce, Mel Torme (opposite Sun sign–Virgo), Jerry Lewis, Red Foxx, Albert Einstein, John Travolta (Aquarius-Pisces cusp, Venus and Mercury in Pisces), Meher Baba, Walter Mondale (Pisces Ascendant), Fats Domino, Magic Johnson (face), Danny DeVito.

TYPE 2: Liz Taylor, Lillian Gish, Tinkerbell, the Little Prince, Alice of *Alice in Wonderland*, PeeWee Herman, Vaslav Nijinski as the Fawn in *Afternoon of the Fawn*, Billie Holiday (Moon, Mars, Venus and Jupiter in Pisces), Botticelli's *Venus*, Judy Garland as Dorothy in *The Wizard of Oz*, Russian dancer Nureyev.

TYPE 3: James Taylor, Kurt Cobain, Ralph Nader, Johnny Cash and George Harrison.

PLANETS

SUN

Madonna, Pavarotti (with Jupiter), Rosanne Cash, Sylvester Stallone, Elvis Presley.

MOON

FULL MOON: Alfred Hitchcock, Louis Armstrong, Mother Goddess figures, Burl Ives, Babe Ruth, Charles Laughton, Roseanne Barr-Arnold, Julian Assange (Cancer Sun, Moon rising).

NEW MOON: Sal Mineo in *Rebel Without a Cause*, PeeWee Herman when sad, Laura Nyro, *Mona Lisa*, Princess Diana.

MERCURY

Michael Jackson, Jack Lemon, Joel Gray, Judy Garland, Prince, Michael Scott, Peter Pan, Sandy Dennis, Michael J. Fox, Mary Tyler Moore, Warner Brother's Tweetie Bird, Reba McIntyre.

VENUS

Boticelli's *Venus*, Elvis Presley, Bing Crosby (Sun and Moon in Venus-ruled signs), Jane Fonda, Henry Fonda, Bernadette Peters (with Mercury), Kewpie Dolls, Caravaggio's *Bacco*, Brigitte Bardot, Oscar Wilde, Fred Astaire, Julie Andrews, Barbara K. Roberts.

MARS

Jillian Michaels (trainer on *The Biggest Loser*), Suze Orman, rocker Melissa Etherdge, and baseball's Mark McGwire.

*TYPE 1:** Glenn Close, Helen Reddy, Ted Dansen, Al Gore, Napoleon, Tom Cruise, Patrick Swayze, Dan Quayle, Gabriella Sabitini, Mike Ditka, Chuck Connors, Judith Light, Bonnie Raitt, Betty Ford (Mars with Jupiter), Geronimo (Mars-Saturn blend).

*TYPE 2:**: James Brown, George Wallace (Gov. AL), Mike Ditka, Archie Bunker, Burt Reynolds, Chuck Connors, Barbara Bush, Dick Butkis, James Cagney, Mickey Rooney (Mars with Mercury).

* *Due to media preference and prejudice, it is very difficult to find outstanding examples of the Mars type and Jupiterian type female among famous entertainers.*

JUPITER

Lyndon Johnson, Burl Ives, The Quaker on the Quaker oatmeal box, James Beard, Jackie Gleason, Pope John Paul, Ben Franklin, Jay Leno, Carole King, Mark Twain (Samuel Clemmons), Mama Cass Elliot, Yogananda, Meher Baba, Buddha.

SATURN

Michelle and Barack Obama, Abraham Lincoln (Sun, Moon, Ascendant in Saturn-ruled signs and Saturn at the Midheaven), J. Krishnamurti, Joan Baez (with Venus), Aubrey Beardsley, Ichabod Crane, Scrooge, Virginia Woolf, Greta Garbo, Clint Eastwood, David Bowie, Barbara Stanwyk, Vita Sackville-West.

OUTER PLANETS

Pay more attention to the "atmosphere" of the outer planets as they reflect at the individual level. The following examples concern mood more than anatomy.

URANUS

The wild-haired scientist, Doc Brown, in *Back to the Future*, comedienne Paula Poundstone, Dwight Schrute of *The Office*.

NEPTUNE

Paula Abdul, Billie Holiday (sad Neptunian), Bing Crosby (cheerful, romantic Neptunian), George Harrison, Edgar Cayce, Oscar Wilde, Marilyn Monroe, Red Foxx.

PLUTO

Anthony Hopkins (portrayal of Hannibal Lecter), Dr. "Death" Kevorkian, Priscilla Presley (very intense), Marlon Brando, Batman, Kojak, the Godfather, Sinéad O'Connor, Rajneesh, Saddam Hussein.

APPENDICES

As Above

...So Below

APPENDIX I
ZODIACAL CORRESPONDENCES TO THE HUMAN BODY

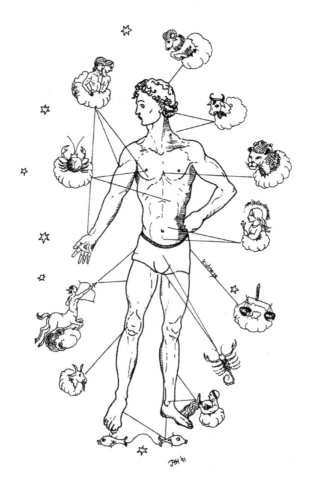

THE ZODIACAL MAN
A general correlation of twelve zodiac signs with the human body

ZODIAC SIGN CORRESPONDENCES
TO THE HUMAN BODY

Aries	Top of head, eyes, upper jaw, upper teeth, brain
Taurus	Lower jaw, lower, teeth, mouth, tongue, ears, neck, tonsils and larynx
Gemini	Shoulders, arms, hands, fingers, lungs, bronchial tubes, clavicles, capilaries
Cancer	Breast, rib cage, stomach, uterus, spleen
Leo	Heart, back, dorsal vertebrae, spinal sheaths
Virgo	Intestines, appendix, abdomen, spleen, lower lobes of the liver, pancreas, immune system
Libra	Kidneys, equilibrium, adrenals (with Aries, Mars), lower back
Scorpio	Genitals, colon, sweat glands, bladder, nose, pelvis, sacrum
Sagittarius	Hips, thighs, sciatic nerve, arteries, buttocks
Capricorn	Knees, bone in general, joints, skin, cuticles, nails
Aquarius	Ankles, shins, Achilles tendon, circulation of the blood, electrical body
Pisces	Feet, toes, lymph, immune system (with Virgo)

APPENDIX II
A REFINEMENT OF
THE TWELVE SIGN TYPES

Each of the 12 zodiac signs is subdivided into three sections of 10°, or "decanates." Traditionally, the physical appearance of each decanate is thought to be a blend of the Sign type with the Sign type attributed to the decanate. All three decanates of a Fire sign will be ruled by Fire signs. Each decanate of an Air sign will be ruled by Air signs, and so forth for the Earth and Water signs.

Sometimes astrologers take the degree of zodiacal longitude rising at birth and attribute the physical characteristics of the decanate that degree belongs to with the physical appearance of the individual. However, the small influence the decanates suggest seems over-ruled in most cases by the several Significators of Physical appearance given in Table 2, page 33. The student may find the following Table 4 interesting and in rare cases useful.

TABLE 4
THE 36 DECANATES

SIGN	0-9.59° 1st Decanate	10-19.59° 2nd Decanate	20-29.59° 3rd Decanate
ARIES	*ARIES*	*LEO*	*SAGITTARIUS*
TAURUS	*TAURUS*	*VIRGO*	*CAPRICORN*
GEMINI	*GEMINI*	*LIBRA*	*AQUARIUS*
CANCER	*CANCER*	*SCORPIO*	*PISCES*
LEO	*LEO*	*SAGITTARIUS*	*ARIES*
VIRGO	*VIRGO*	*CAPRICORN*	*TAURUS*
LIBRA	*LIBRA*	*AQUARIUS*	*GEMINI*
SCORPIO	*SCORPIO*	*PISCES*	*CANCER*
SAGITTARIUS	*SAGITTARIUS*	*ARIES*	*LEO*
CAPRICORN	*CAPRICORN*	*TAURUS*	*VIRGO*
AQUARIUS	*AQUARIUS*	*GEMINI*	*LIBRA*
PISCES	*PISCES*	*CANCER*	*SCORPIO*

APPENDIX III
REDHEADS AND MARS*

For over 2,000 years astrologers have associated the red planet Mars with redheaded people. The fact that Mars was the ancient god of war is reflected in our popular belief in hot-tempered redheads. Writing in 140 C.E., Ptolemy states that "Mars ascending gives a fair ruddiness to the person...and the hair of the head light or red...."[1] [*Notes follow on page 197*] This was echoed centuries later by Sepharial's "...Mars exactly rising produces red hair."[2] Presented here are the startling results of "The Redheads Research Project," an international project designed to test the validity of the astrological tradition that Mars should be exceptionally strong in the birth charts of naturally redheaded people.

MEDICAL ANOMALIES AND THE MARS-REDHEAD LINK
A great deal of prejudice and superstition surrounds redheaded people, especially in Europe. Redheads are thought to be alternately lucky and unlucky, over-sexed, temperamental, angry, possessed of psychic powers, witches, etc. Ancient Syrians sacrificed redheaded men in honor of Mars. But really, is there anything actually different about redheaded people? And is there anything that might link them to "their" patron, Mars?

Yes, there actually are some physical-medical facts about redheads that set them apart as a population. And yes, these medical anomalies do relate, via the tradition of medical astrology, to the planet Mars. First, red hair is red because of a superabundance of *trichosiderin,* a chemical compound made partly of iron and found *only* in red hair. Astrological texts state clearly that the metal iron is under the rulership of Mars. Therefore, blacksmiths, iron

* *First published as an article in* The Mountain Astrologer, *May, 1996.*

tools, and anything else related to iron is held to be under the dominion of the red planet. Curiously too, the part of the birth chart most often associated in the Western astrological tradition with the head and face is the Ascendant, or Rising Point. Mars found in the vicinity of the Ascendant at birth has traditionally been associated with red hair.

Anybody can have freckles. However it is also true that redheads are uniquely disposed to freckling. Here is what Cornell's Medical Encyclopedia has to say: "Freckles are due principally to a predominance of iron in the skin (iron ruled by Mars), and Mars prominent at birth; Mars in the Ascendant, or Rising, or a Mars influence or sign on the Ascendant. Mars rising in Aries tends to give a face full of freckles and fiery red hair...."

As iron equals Mars, it seems as though our astrological language of affinities allows us to transpose "Mars rising" as "iron about the head."

Secondly, redheaded children are more likely than average to be hyperactive. Pediatrician Lendon Smith reports that an unusually high percentage of hyperactive children are redheaded, based on a study he conducted of 8,000 hyperactive children. Symptoms of hyperactivity include excitability, inappropriate aggression, disdain for affectionate conduct, and abnormal activity. It would be fair to associate such traits with Mars, particularly when in excess.

Medical astrology assigns the blood (red corpuscles and hemoglobin) to the rulership of Mars. Curiously, many red-haired people suffer from extended bleeding due to delayed blood clotting! Anthropologist Ashley Montague cites that "There is some evidence that the bleeding time of redheads is longer than that for brunettes and blondes. Some obstetricians take special precautions when a redheaded woman is to be delivered of a baby because of the tendency of some redheads to bleed profusely following delivery.

Although the ancients probably conducted no statistical tests for hyperactivity in redheads, nor knew that an iron compound (trichosiderin) was causative to red hair, they "coincidentally" selected a patron planet for redheads whose traditional rulerships include some items peculiar to redhead populations. Could they have arrived at their choice of Mars through the observation of the planetary birth charts of redheaded people? Perhaps we will never really know. What we do know is the area of the horoscope nearest the Rising or Ascendant degree has long been associated with physical appearance.

Should Mars "rule" redheads, as tradition holds, then Mars should be prominent in some way in the charts of redheaded people. Pioneered by Judith A. Hill and Jacalyn Thompson's first findings in "The Mars-Redhead Link," collectors in four separate world locations have worked to collect the birth data of naturally redheded people. To date, over 1,452 birth charts of redheaded people have been collected, representing the collection efforts of research teams (described later): two American, one Canadian, and one English-Scottish. **This international scale research of Mars distribution in redhead populations constitutes the largest collaborative astro-genetic research project ever concluded, and thus signals an accomplishment of historic importance for astrology.** The results of Hill and Thompson's first study and the ensuing two world replication projects will be detailed later in this article. First, however, I would like to pose and answer the questions most frequently asked about the Redheads Research Project.

COMMONLY ASKED QUESTIONS

Why are you studying redheads?

Redheadedness was selected as a topic of research for the following reasons:

1) Red hair is the result of a specific genetic trait. This fact makes for more precise research, since psychological factors can be eliminated. Psychological, cultural, and environmental factors

do not produce redheads and, therefore, objections to this project based on these three factors can be disregarded.

2) Red hair is both rare and noticeable. An estimated 5 percent of the North American population is redheaded.

3) Astrologers have reported that definite astrological conditions have a tendency to prevail at the time a redheaded person is born (i.e., a very strong Mars).[1]

White mice can be born with Mars is near the Rising Point and yet they are white, not red. Therefore, is not the whole premise of your research rather silly?

Planetary placement reflects what is *possible*. White mice do not have red hair, because this trait does not exist in their gene pool. However, should Mars be strong in their planetary birth map, it is possible for white mice to possess any number of other Martian physical traits available in their genetic pattern. In human beings, a prominent birth Mars might reflect a wide array of possible physical and/or emotional expressions such as wiry hair, moles, aquiline nose, aggression, mechanical ability, etc. Those born with a prominent Mars will not have red hair unless this is a genetic possibility.

Are you saying that a prominent birth Mars actually causes red hair?

No. Planetary placements at birth *reflect*, but do not cause, genetic traits, however, according to the late and esteemed scientist Michel Gauquelin, it is possible for certain genetic populations to prefer birth when specific planets are in certain sectors of the horoscope. He hypothesized the existence of internal "cosmic clocks," allowing certain genetic types of an *in utero* sensitivity to the motion of specific planets, thus triggering the onset of parturition. Gauquelin also discovered that to some extent this planetary sensitivity was shared between parents and offspring. The amazing work of Michel and Francoise Gauquelin is beyond the scope of this article. However, those interested will find the material in the "References" (pages 199 – 200) to be of interest.

My hair is red, and Mars was not near the Rising Point when I was born. Does this invalidate your research?

No one has ever hypothesized or concluded that all redheads must be born with Mars near the Rising. **Redheads can be, and are born with Mars in all astrological house placements.** The idea here is only that a somewhat higher percentage of redheads than non-redheads (of shared ethnicity) will be born with Mars so near the Rising. Also, there are other astrological houses that Mars seems to prefer in the birth charts of redheaded people (such as the late 8th and 9th equal-house sectors). Conversely, there are regions where Mars appears weaker for redheads, for example the equal 7th and 4th houses. In fact, there appears to be an entire signature "redhead curve" for Mars distribution in redhead births through the twelve equal houses! Study the graphics and you will get the picture.

Since red hair occurs mostly in Caucasians, isn't your study of redheads racist?

Naturally redheaded people of several racial backgrounds are included in our data pool. However, it is true that red hair is overwhelmingly a Caucasian phenomenon. A study of Mars distribution in redhead (largely Caucasian) populations is no more racist than a study of menopause in women would be sexist.

What other kinds of astrological similarities (besides Mars rising) have you been finding in the birth charts of natural redheads?

First of all, Mars is almost always prominent in some way. The scientific method forced Jackie and I to limit our original research to within our "Strong Zone" for Mars, which is 30° on either side of the Ascendant. Also common were Mars on critical degrees, Mars in the late 8th and 9th equal houses, and/or Mars strong in several ways simultaneously (ruling the Ascendant and also conjunct the Sun, or in Scorpio). Preliminary research reveals that redheads show some preference for Moon in Fire signs or Capricorn and Ascendant in Cancer/Capricorn (sensitive skin?). Other favored combinations involve the Martian signs (Scorpio, Aries), Fire signs (Aries, Leo, Sagittarius), Mars exaltation (Capricorn), and/or a prominent Mars, Sun or Uranus, especially in association with critical degrees, Ascendant, or the Ascendant ruler.

THE HILL AND THOMPSON STORY: 500 REDHEADS REVISITED

Redheads Research was founded in Berkeley, California by myself in 1987. Soon after Jacalyn Thompson joined the project and we began to collect the first 100 redhead birth charts. Our goal was to collect 500 redhead birth charts within the year. Results— first witnessed by the National Council for Geocosmic Research on May 1, 1987—were encouraging. Based on our pilot results, we formulated and notarized our hypotheses. [Readers interested in conducting your own research beware! **Always notarize** your hypothesis before you proceed to collect data.]

The Redheads Research hypotheses were as follows:

1) "A significant number of naturally redheaded people will be born when Mars is within 30° of the Rising Point. This area encompasses our hypothetical zone for Mars' strength at the time of birth." [See Figure 1, following page.] We dubbed this region the Strong Zone for Mars at birth, which can be seen to incorporate the equal 1st and 12th houses of the horoscope.

2) "A significant number of naturally redheaded people will not be born when Mars is within 30° of the Setting Point. This area represents our hypothetical zone for Mars' weakness at the time of birth." We called this region the "Weak Zone" for Mars distribution at birth in redheads.

3) "The birth charts of random populations of non-redheaded people will show no unusual distribution of Mars in either of the above sections."

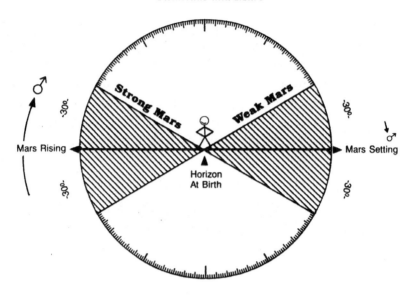

FIGURE 1   ♂ Mars

ASTONISHING RESULTS

We (Hill and Thompson) completed the collection of our goal of 500 redhead birth charts in 1988. The initial findings of statistical consultant Gary Antonacci were highly significant. Exactly 27.2 pecrent of the 500 redheads tested were born when Mars was within 30° of the Rising Point, or within our suggested Strong Zone. Males with bright red hair were born 30 percent of the time with Mars so placed. Three non-redheaded control groups demonstrated that what is normal in the population at large, stands somewhere between 16.9 percent and 19.4 percent. The probability of the redhead result occurring randomly is less than once chance in one million.

Conversely, a low 9.8 percent of the redhead group were born when Mars was within 30° of the Setting Point (Descendant) and within the hypothetical zone for Mars weakness. This percentage for non-redheads, or the population at large, stands between 14.0 and 18.6 percent. The probability of the redhead Weak Zone result occurring randomly is less than one chance in 350,000.

THE MARS-REDHEAD LINK UNDER FIRE

Vehement critics Geoffrey Dean (Australia) and Francoise Gauquelin suggested that these results must be caused by "astronomical factors." The two proposed that our results were due exclusively to Francoise Gauquelin's discovery, the "nycthemeral curve," i.e. the natural variation of the birth Sun position through the twelve "Gauquelin sectors," due to the slightly uneven preference for birth in early morning hours, and thusly the fact that Mars spends more time near the Sun, than opposite.

However, this artifact is only very slight in all Control Groups (0.50-3.0 percent) and therefore could not account for the unusual sector variations for Mars distribution as shown amongst the redhead samples. The strikingly obvious peaks and valleys for Mars distribution in redhead populations are consistent enough to entitle this phenomenon "The Redhead Curve."

Compare Figure 3 "Mars Curves for Redheads," with Figure 4. Control Groups. In response to our critics, we designed a neutral environment for the statistical retesting of the 500 redheads. Full statistical details of these tests are recorded in *The Mars-Redhead Files* by Judith Hill.

Beverly Steffert, Ph.D. and Michael O'Neill, B.Sc., two highly esteemed British researchers, agreed by written contract to retest the Hill-Thompson redhead data. Critics Dean and Gauquelin were invited to submit their statistical testing requests and requirements to Steffert and O'Neill. Francoise Gauquelin accepted the invitation, and her data-testing requests were carried out in full by Mike O'Neill under the direction of Beverly Steffert.

Steffert and O'Neill found that our claims held true. The fantastically high incidence of Mars near the Rising Point for redheads at birth was not due to any of the "astronomical factors" proposed by critics of the study. Beverly Steffert concluded her review, "The Mars-Redhead Link Under Attack" with several important statements, including:

"This data has been quite rigorously scrutinized by now. As reported, on the figures provided, there is no case for rejecting the authors' claim. There hypotheses were upheld. But the many provisos that need to be added mean that the next step can only be replication, using a new sample of redheads, if possible, from another country. One more reason to accept the redhead/ Mars hypothesis is that astrologer John Addey had collected the charts of 100 redheads some 20 years ago with his own Martian hypothesis in mind. [11] Although the data was not significant, the same trend was evident—an excess at the rise and a deficit at the set. The implications of this study are so astounding to the average skeptic (that planetary activity may influence genetic expression of a physical objectively measurable trait) that replication is essential…."

PLAY IT AGAIN SAM

No matter how good the result, the scientific method demands "replication," or a repetition of your first result. Acknowledging the necessity for replication, we (Hill and Thompson) actually collected our 500 redhead birth charts in *five* groups of 100 birth charts. This means that our first pilot study of 100 redheads had already been succeeded by four successful replications. This important fact was conveniently ignored by critics of the project, who insisted on viewing our five redhead "samples" as but one group of 500 redheads. We were advised to "replicate" our "first" results. It was back to the drawing board for the Redheads Project.

In the United Kingdom, an English-Scottish replication of effort was spearheaded by Beverly Steffert and Mike O'Neill. The two collected the birth data of 373 new Scottish and English redheads. Additionally, Charles Harvey graciously provided Hill and Thompson the fascinating research notes, completed over 20 years ago, of astrologer John Addey, which detailed Mars positions at birth (angularity to the Ascendant) for 100 British redheads. This group was enormously important, as its existence was unknown to

Hill or Thompson at the time of their project design, hypothesis formation, or data collection in America twenty years later.

Simultaneously, back in the United States, 23 volunteers, under my direction, collected 374 redhead data points, collected 374 redhead data points. These data points were submitted in sealed envelopes, later to be opened, signed and numbered before two witnesses, and then hurried as raw data to Mike O'Neill in England for computer entry. (In this manner, I avoided "contaminating" my data with my own speculatively biased involvement.) Canada's contribution of the birth data of 29 "bright redheaded females" was submitted to Redheads Research by astrologer Ron Bippus. This tiny but important group constitutes the only sample of Canadian redheads extant. An additional 75 "strawberry blonde" data points were entered by Hill and Thompson, left over as a subsample from our original study. The set of strawberry blonde data points were mailed as raw data to Mike O'Neill in London for first computer entry and viewing of results. This gave a total of 479 American Continent Replication Redheads.

THE REDHEAD DATA

The extensive details of these replication samples, and of their collectors and collection methodology, are described exhaustively in my article "The Mars-Redhead Link II: Mars Distribution Patterns in Redhead Populations," in *Borderlands (Volume LI, Nos. 1 and 2)*. Presented below are the greater combined redhead data groups:

Redhead Group A: 500 Hill-Thompson American Redheads;

Redhead Group B: 1,452 Total World Redheads;

Redhead Group C: 979 Total American-Canadian Redheads;

Redhead Group D: 479 Total American-Canadian Replication Redheads;

Redhead Group E: 473 Total English-Scottish Replication Redheads

(Note: **Group E** contains 373 data points appearing with the per-

mission of Mike O'Neill on a highly provisional basis only, the additional 100 U.K. data points are from John Addey.]

Redhead Group F: 952 Total World Redhead Replication data.

Groups **D**, **E** and **F** contain only "new" redhead data and no original Hill and Thompson data. Therefore, these three replication groups are of central importance in the testing for any repeating effects of the Hill and Thompson study.

The Control Groups Represent the Expected Mars Distributions: First, what is the expected number of Mars positions at birth within Hill and Thompson's Strong and Weak zones for the population at large? What about for non-redheads or, more specifically, for any *purely random* groups of birthdays? To know this, you must first establish adequate comparisons, better known as "controls." Mark Pottenger has been of inestimable value in the design of two nearly ideal controls for comparison with each of the above redhead groups **A-F**. These controls are:

Control Group 1 (C 1): An astronomical control. The basic distribution by zodiacal angle from the Rising Point (Ascendant) at the mean latitude for each redhead group.

Control Group 2 (C 2): An Astrodemographic or "time-switched" control. The date, year and place of birth for each redhead in each redhead group is maintained, and only the *times switched*. This provides a demographically perfect "random" control population for comparison with the redhead group in question. (Actually, Mark's process was a good deal more complex than this, involving multiple time-switches, etc., and will be described in an upcoming technical research report.) See Tables 1 and 2 for a comparison of statistical/numerical results for redhead groups **A-F** and control groups **C 1** and **C 2**.

WHAT STATISTICAL SIGNIFICANCE MEANS

Both critics and supporters of the Mars-redhead link were

eager to learn one thing: Would the new redhead groups reproduce the same results as the Hill-Thompson redheads? In other words, would the new groups produce enough Mars positions within 30° of the Ascendant to qualify in scientific circles as statistically "significant"?

MARS DISTRIBUTION
Redheads vs Controls

Mars distribution at birth within 30° of the Ascendant, (Strong Zone). Total Mars occurrence for Redhead groups (A,D, E, G, F, B) compared to the *expected* occurrence as established by Mark Pottenger's two controls (individually developed for comparison with each redhead group). Below, the total Mars distributions for both the Redheads and Controls, Chi squares, Probability values.

Redhead Groups	REDHEADS Strong Zone (total frequency)	CONTROLS Strong Zone (rounded to highest)	Chi square	Probability (n=1)
A:500 Am	136	86	28.54	9.18E-08
Redheads		89	25.18	5.22E-07
D:479 Am-Cn	105	82	6.64	0.0099
Replic. Reds		87	3.88	0.048
E:373 UK	71	64	n.s.	n.s.
Replic. Reds		66	n.s.	n.s.
E:100 UK	21	17	n.s.	n.s.
F:952 World	197	163	7.14	0.007
Replic. Reds		169	5.90	0.015
B:1452 Total	333	249	28.15	1.12E-07
World Reds		258	21.46	3.61E-06

Table 1

Significance is a measurement of the odds that an experimental population differs from the population as a whole. Very loosely, statistical significance is commonly held to be achieved when the probability of any pre-hypothesized phenomenon (in our case, Mars in the Strong zone) as only one chance in 20 of occurring by chance factors alone. Thus, a probability of .05 (or P+.05) is the number needed to get the ball in the hoop, so to speak. One chance in 10, or P=.10 is thought to be "nearly significant" or very good, and anything less than that is simply a waste of time, from the standpoint of many statisticians.

Tedious statistical discussion leaves most people cold. For you statistics buffs, I've included the probability in the far right column of Table 1. I've also included all Mars distributions for redheads and controls, should you feel inclined to test my results for yourselves. For the rest of you, be assured that the statistical description here is brief, and we will soon be on to more exciting things.

REDHEADS REPLICATION RESULTS

We already know that Redhead Group **A** (Hill and Thompson's 500 redheads) was statistically significant in regards to Mars distribution within 30° of the Ascendant. Hill and Thompson's idea of an alternate Weak Zone for redhead groups, in which Mars distribution at birth was located within 30° of the Descendant, also held true. So, are the new replication Redhead Groups **D**, **E** and **F** statistically significant? And is **B**, the total 1,452 World Redheads, significant? *Yes, with the single exception of the British Redheads (E) all new large combined redhead groups achieved levels of significance within Hill-Thompson's Strong Zone at the level of P=.05 or above.* This includes two of three groups containing absolutely no original Hill-Thompson data.

Interestingly, the one failing group, **E**, produced results "in the correct direction of the hypothesis" by outperforming all controls for Mars distribution within the Strong Zone (see Tables 1 and 2). Therefore, group **E** contributes to the significance achieved for group **F**. The Total 952 World replication data, and also for **B**, Total 1,452 World Redheads. The American-Canadian replication group (**D**) and also the Total World Replication group (**F**) are indeed significant, although not at the fantastically high levels shown for Hill and Thompson's first redheads (see Table 1). Remaining groups B and C do contain the original Hill and Thompson data, and therefore produce highly significant results.

THE STRONG/WEAK ZONE VARIATION
REDHEADS VS TWO CONTROLS
This Table gives the *difference between* Mars distribution
at birth within 30 degrees of the Asc. (Strong Zone) and also
within 30 degrees of the Desc. (Weak Zone). All redhead
groups (A-F) are compared with two controls developed
for each group by Mark Pottenger: (C1,C2)

Redhead Groups	REDHEADS	CONTROLS: (C1,C2) (Expected Frequency)
A:500 Am Redheads	88.00	6.37 (C1) 10.50 (C2)
B:1352 Ttl. World Reds	135.00	13.85 23.34
C:979 Ttl. Am-Cn Reds	121.00	9.93 23.34
D:479Am-Cn Replic. Reds	33.00	3.65 12.41
E:373 British Replic. Reds	16.00	3.52 6.86
G:100 Addey	7.00	1.90 .89
F:852 World Replication	49.00	7.58 12.85

Table 2

Statistical significance increases when a trend shown for a small group continues on as the group increases in size. Both the British and American replication redheads data sets (**D** and E) are composed of two or more sub-samples (detailed in the Borderlands article). Redhead Group **F** is comprised of all possible world replication studies. Total replication redheads (**F**) were significant for Mars at birth in Hill and Thompson's Strong Zone at between seven chances in 10,000, using **C 1**, and three chances in 200, using **C 2** (see Table 1).

With so much evidence at had, it is now possible to assert (tentatively) that redhead groups do indeed produce higher levels of Mars distribution within 30° of the Ascendant than do non-redheads, or the population at large. Individual redhead groups vary in this respect from being nearly significant, or "in the right direction of the hypothesis," to be extremely significant. Again, the statistical enthusiast can find these figures in Tables 1 and 2. However, my claims are necessarily cautious. Results may always be overturned by new results, and the scientific process is ongoing.

Curiously, the Weak Zone failed to obtain significant results for any group. however, most groups do indeed demonstrate lower distributions than the controls, sometimes significantly so, in at least one-half of the Weak Zone (i.e., the equal 7th or the equal 6th house). Certainly, some sort of Weak Zone for Mars distribution can be seen to occur within 30° of the Descendant, but unreliably so, and varying widely between redhead groups.

A DRAMATIC FINDING

And now, the most striking discovery of this study. The real surprise lies not with the high Mars distribution near the Ascendant, where Mars rises, but *between* the Ascendant and the Descendant, where Mars sets. For all redhead groups, the difference between these two zones is enormous, *many times* what is seen for control groups [see figures 2, 3, 4 and Table 2]. If you subtract the number of Mars occurrences within the Weak Zone from the number of Mars occurrences within the Strong Zone, you will obtain a figure. Let us call this figure Total Strong Weak Zone Difference.

As you can readily see from Table 2, redheads significantly outperform control groups, who show very little variance between the two zones (see Figure 4). It is impossible to ignore the fact that for whatever reason, redheads produce wildly different trends in Mars distribution than do non-redheads. Statistical tests need to be developed for assessing the probability of this exciting phenomenon. The extremity of the effect should guarantee a high level of statistical significance.

TWO AMERICAN CONTINENT REDHEAD GROUPS:
MARS DISTRIBUTION THROUGH TWELVE ASTRO-
LOGICAL EQUAL HOUSE SECTORS. (Layout begins with
the 4th equal house sector.)
A: 500 American redheads (J.Hill and J. Thompson).
D: 479 American-Canadian (Redheads Research).
Baseline: mean house distribution is 8.33 of sample per house.
Expected frequencies vary per sector by no greater than 0.50.

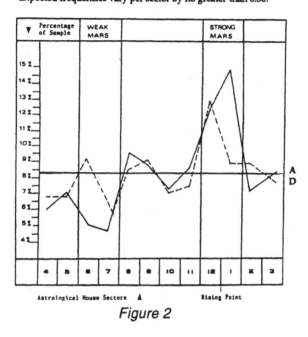

Figure 2

THE MYSTERIOUS REDHEAD CURVE

Perhaps the single most puzzling discovery is the appearance
of what may well be a recognizable redhead curve for Mars
distribution throughout all twelve equal houses. This observation
is explicated in the *Borderlands* article. It is important to add
that after viewing the first 500 redheads, I hypothesized that in
subsequent redhead collections, their unique twelve-house Martian
curve pattern would replicate with variations of no more than 30°.
This prediction was sent to three eminent researchers within the
astrological community and accompanied by a graphic depiction
of the hypothesized redhead-curve pattern, developed after viewing

the Mars-distribution patterns of the Hill-Thompson and Addey redhead data. This was accomplished prior to my witnessing the Mars curves for the new replication data groups **D, E** and **F**.

THE GRAPHICS

Three figures are provided showing the birth incidence of Mars through the twelve equal house sectors. The Martian curve through these twelve houses is shown for both redheads (Figures 2 and 3) and their controls (Figure 4). The reader should note that Figures 2, 3 and 4 display the twelve equal astrological houses as starting with the 4th equal house. This somewhat untraditional layout best displays for viewing purposes the Strong and Weak Zones for Mars distribution at birth in redhead and random populations. So just what should a normal Martian birth curve for any population at large look like? Figure 4 displays the controls, or the *expected* Mars birth curve, for purely random populations.

A VISUAL APPROACH TO MARS DISTRIBUTION

Do Mars-distribution curves through the twelve equal astrological houses look different for redhead groups than for their controls? Do Mars-distribution curves for different redhead groups resemble each other? As space is limited here, I would like to invite the reader to judge for him/herself. The tools we need are provided by Figures 2, 3 and 4. My approach here will be strictly visual (supported by two numerical/statistical tables, for those so inclined).

In the physical sciences, such as physical anthropology, geology, or genetics, a straight-forward visual observation has never been entirely abandoned to numbers! (Your second generation pea plants either possess the yellow stripe their parent did or not.) Parapsychological studies, for example, make frequent use of comparisons of drawings, cards, etc., in addition to statistical analysis. However, astrological researchers of our era have preferred

TWO UK REDHEAD GROUPS: MARS DISTRIBUTIONS AT
BIRTH THROUGH THE TWELVE ASTROLOGICAL EQUAL
HOUSE SECTORS. (layout begins with the 4th equal house.)
E: 373 UK Redheads (B.Steffert Ph.D. and M.O'Neill B.Sc.).
G: 100 UK Redheads (J. Addey, collected in 1960s).
Baseline: mean house distribution is 8.33 of sample per house.
Expected frequencies vary per sector by no greater than 0.50 .

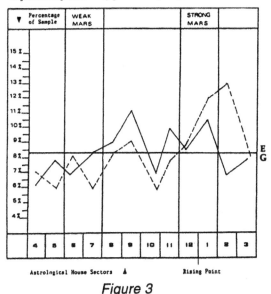

Figure 3

an almost purely statistical approach. This is unfortunate, because
statistics do not always provide an adequate view of a visually
obvious phenomenon.

John Addey was one of the few respected astrological
researchers who utilized (in part) a holistic curve-wave model in
the study of planetary distributions for various groups. Today,
we find that unusual or even startling planetary distribution
patterns are ignored in favor of the popular statistical analysis. For
instance, a statistician would say that redheads (**E**, Figure 3) were
insignificant in the Strong and Weak Zones, and stop there. This
conclusive sounding statement misleads one to suppose that there
is nothing unusual about the strongly angular English redhead's
distribution curve for Mars, and that the Martian curves for
English redhead groups must, therefore, be identical to those of

their controls. However, you can see for yourself in Figure 4 that the control group curves are not angular at all, but nearly flat.

Although statistics are indispensable for many purposes, on one hand they can fail to describe total holistic pictures. On the other hand, a visual approach is direct. In other words: *Do two Mars-distribution curves look alike, or don't they? And: Can you, the reader, tell the difference between a redhead curve and a control curve?*

To answer the first question, the reader should compare Figures 2 and 3 (redheads) with Figure 4 (control groups). Please keep in mind that the control curves depicted by Figure 4 show the expected distribution of Mars at birth. An even casual look tells us that the two American Continent redhead groups of Figure 2 and the two U.K. redhead groups of Figure 3 produce highly angular Martian curve-waves that look nothing like the flat control groups, but very much like each other! *If there is nothing to this business of a Mars-redhead link, then there should be no discernible difference between the redhead distributions shown by Figures 2 and 3 and the controls of Figure 4.*

COMPARING THE VISUAL IMAGES CLOSELY

Let us explore more deeply the Mars-distribution curves for redheads and controls. Notice how the controls (Figure 4) are nearly flat, with only a slight rise between the 11th and 12th equal houses—near and in Hill and Thompson's Strong Zone! This is due to what Francoise Gauquelin has coined the "nycthemeral" curve for Mars distribution. Gauquelin discovered that babies prefer, by a small margin, to be born in the wee hours. Therefore, more people are born with the Sun in the eastern skies than in the west. Mars also is more commonly found near the Sun that farther away. The result? A standard excess of Mars, *not exceeding one percent*, is seen in the Strong Zone as compared to Hill and Thompson's Weak Zone.

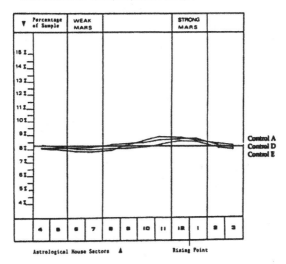

MARS DISTRIBUTION THROUGH TWELVE
EQUAL HOUSE SECTORS (for comparison
with Figures 2 and 3 (UK Redheads and American Continent Redheads).

Control A: Astro-demographic control created
from time switching Am.Redhead group A. (Fig 2)
Control D: Astro-demographic control created
from time-switching Am.Redhead group D. (Fig 2)
Control E: Astro-demographic group created
from time-switching UK Redhead group E. (Fig 3)
These Controls are developed by Mark Pottenger.

Figure 4

However, this does not explain the substantial redhead excess
in the Strong Zone. You can see for yourself that all redhead groups
produce Mars distributions within either the equal 1st or 12th
houses (half-zones of the Strong Zones) or the entire zone itself to
exceed that sown for all control populations. Let us now compare
redhead Figures 2 and 3 with control Figure 4.

Although nearly flat, the control curve rises steadily through
the 10th and 11th equal houses. Not so the redheads. Redhead
curves demonstrate several distribution anomalies consistent
among themselves and unseen in random groups such as those
shown in Figure 4. First of all, redheads demonstrate an enormous
difference between Weak Zone and Strong Zone distribution. The

skeptic might well think this is some kind of trick. However, this phenomenon holds true on any scale the graphics are placed, and also shows up numerically (Table 2). To date, all redhead groups show this phenomenon.

Redheads also display gross differences, as compared to controls, between their second highest peak (8th–9th equal houses) and their second lowest dip (10 equal house). A similar variance lies between the 10th equal house (low) and the Strong Zone (high). *The reader can now see how the redhead curve falls sharply at two points and rises sharply at two points.* The controls do no such thing. In fact the control distribution rises between the 9th and 11th, which is exactly opposite the redhead trend. Now it becomes evident why a visual examination of the data is so important. Nearly (but not all) of these holistically viewed findings are overlooked through use of a purely statistical approach.

Visually, the angular-looking Mars-distribution pattern of American redheads (Figure 2) holds much in common with the British redhead pattern (Figure 3). I maintain that any ten-year-old child could select these redhead curves as "more related" to each other than to the nearly flat-looing controls. However, there are some important differences between American and British curves. Firstly, the American redhead data holds up under statistical scrutiny for Mars incidence within the Strong Zone and the British data does not. Secondly, the larger British group (E, Steffert and O'Neill) displays a significant distribution in the equal 9th house. (Although American groups rise slightly above the mean in this region, they do not do so at a statistically significant level.) Finally, within the Strong Zone itself, the British redheads prefer the equal 1st house, and the Americans are divided. Hill and Thompson's original 500 redheads (A) were very strong in both sectors of the Strong Zone—the 1st and 12th equal houses. The 479 American replication redheads (D) show a significant incidence of Mars distribution only in the equal 12th house, at a level equal to Hill and Thompson's first redheads.

THE UNSOLVED MYSTERIES

There are many unanswered questions and this work is yet nascent. First, why does Mars appear to favor certain equal house sectors within the circle of diurnal motion for a population sharing a specific genetic trait? How does this relate genetics with astrological rhythms? Could it be that specific genetic traits are reflected collectively in genetic signature curves for whole populations sharing the trait? Or, rather, is it as Michel Gauquelin hypothesized, that some groups inherit biological clocks sensitive to the motion of specific planets and therefore birth when these planets transit preferred sectors of the diurnal wheel? And if this is so, then would not interference or changes in the Earth's magnetic field as influenced by latitude, longitude, season, sunspots, or weather compromise the sensitivity of such internal clocks? Could this account fore the variation in results seen between some of the recent British redheads and the American-Canadian, as well as the earlier-era John Addey British redheads?

A DARING ASTRO-GENETIC THEORY

In scientific research it is advisable to encourage what appears to be the most daring ideas.–D'Arsonval

The experiments of chemist Lily Kolisko (1920s–1960s) suggest that metals in solution can be observed to respond to specific astrological conditions, i.e., conjunctions of their *traditionally associated planet* with the Moon. These ancient planet-metal correspondences are as follows: Mars=iron, Venus=copper, Mercury=mercury, Jupiter=tin, Saturn=lead, Sun=gold and Moon=silver. It is only the Mars=iron correspondence that concerns us here.

When mixed with silver nitrate, ferrous sulfate (iron) will form interesting designs on dipped filter paper. In fact, each metal in solution will create "signature" designs unique to themselves. Following the intuition of Dr. Rudolf Steiner, Lily Kolisko discovered that just after the Moon's exact conjunction with Mars, the otherwise predictable ferrous sulfate designs would all but disappear. Similar results were obtained with ferrous sulfate for Mars-Saturn conjunctions, lead for Saturn-Moon conjunctions, and with gold chloride for solar eclipses. Similar results were later obtained by Dr. Rudolf Hauschka (1949), Theodore Schwenk (1949), Karl Voss (1964), Agnes Fife (1967) and Michael Drummond (1976).

So, what does this have to do with the curious effects for Mars distribution in redheads at birth as witnessed by these research studies? As stated earlier, red hair is red because of the presence of an abundance of trichosiderin, a chemical compound made partly of iron and found only in red hair. Perhaps in utero, redheads through an unknown mechanism of iron conductivity to the movements of Mars much as does ferrous sulfate to Mars' conjunction with the Moon. An outlandish theory? Perhaps. And yet, why and how the unique Mars-redhead distribution curve occurs will no doubt entail some interesting, if not far out, speculations! *In light of this idea, we could theorize that the metabolism, brain waves, and/or other bio-electrical activity would increase in naturally redheaded individuals as Mars transited within 30° of the Ascendant each day, and would decrease as it closely transited the Descendant. This effect would be most noticeable for redheads who were born with Mars transiting within 30° of their exact Ascendant.*

We know that males possess more iron in their bodies than females and that females have more copper in their bodies than males. Curiously, today's medical books still use the astrological symbol for Mars to denote male gender and Venus for female. The metal connections to physical types appear to be very ancient. Perhaps each of the traditional planetary types will be found to either possess or be more responsive to their traditionally assigned metal than the norm. It would be interesting to view the Gauquelin heredity experiments in the light of planet-metal types. According to Gauquelin, parents and their children were more likely than chance factors alone would permit to share at birth the same planets in key Gauquelin sectors of the horoscope. Do parents and their children who share, for example, a similar birth placement of Venus also share Venus' motion via a physical abundance of Venus' metal, copper?

Of course, we all have some iron in our bodies, and it would be silly to think that redheads somehow corner the market on an iron-based responsiveness to Mars! Other groups, such as top achieving athletes, doctors and generals have been demonstrated by Michel and Francoise Gauquelin to possess birth distribution curves for Mars unique to themselves and not occurring in random populations. Athletes, generals and doctors require a very strong Mars, certainly from the astrologer's perspective.

The graphic evidence here does not imply that non-redheads have no "Mars responsiveness" at birth, but rather that redheads, when viewed as a group, possess a sort of signature Mars response visible as a distinctive redhead Mars-distribution curve. (One might note that the redhead curve differs from Martian birth curves associated by the Gauquelins with specific vocational groups. This is beyond the scope of this article.) Apparently, redheads prefer to make their first appearances on the stage of life when Mars transits certain equal house sectors of the birth chart, while avoiding other sectors.

If astrology works, then physical anomaly must reflect itself— no matter how subtly—in the planetary patterns of those who possess this specific genetic trait. It would seem that the research of astro-genetic correlations would be one of the most fruitful routes open to astrologers who are hopeful of "proving" astrology's validity to the skeptical inquirer. John Addey put it very well by stating that order by its very nature is distinguished by law: one cannot have order appearing and maintaining itself by chance. It is to the discovery of these laws of genetic astrology that we suggest astrologers should now be addressing themselves (*Harmonics*).

SUMMARY

Visually, the strongly angular Mars-distribution curves for all redhead groups do not resemble Mark Pottenger's nearly flat astronomical and time-switched controls, Rather, they resemble each other so strongly that a child can readily segregate redhead curve signatures from those of their controls, as could any rational adult. This means that redhead groups, when compared to controls, produce exaggerated high and ow distributions for Mars within the twelve equal houses of the birth chart. In contrast, random or non-redhead groups show little variance of Mars distribution through the twelve equal astrological houses at birth.

Three statements best summarize my findings:

1) Mars distribution at birth for redheads groups through the twelve equal astrological houses is not identical to that of purely random populations;

2) Redhead groups produce visually similar and strongly angular Martian distribution signatures through the twelve equal astrological houses that are highly anomalous in contrast to the nearly flat appearance of the control population Mars-distribution signatures; and

3. Redheads show a higher incidence of Mars within 30° of the Ascendant (on either or both sides) than do control populations. This difference will vary between redhead groups, sometimes being merely "higher" than controls, and in many cases significantly so.

Perhaps Ptolemy was on to something after all.

EPILOGUE

Redhead research has submitted all data collected under its auspices to outside neutral testing. Past participants in data examination and testing are: Gary Antonacci, Robert Wambach Ph.D., Mike O'Neill B.Sc., Beverly Steffert Ph.D., Lee Lehman Ph.D., and Mark Pottenger. The original Hill and Thompson data was released into the public domain in 1995, and is now in the possession of three data banks: Astrolabe (USA), AstroCalc

(England), and the data bank of the German Astrological Society.

The American Redheads Replication Project data is still undergoing testing and will be released in 1997, following (and dependent upon) the adequate publication of final results.[12]

NOTES

1. Claudius Ptolemy, *Tetrobiblios*, 140 c.e., Book the Third Chapter 16, the Form and Temperament of the Body: "Mars ascending gives a fair ruddiness to the person…and the hair of the head light or red…."

2. Sepharial, *The Manual of Astrology*, New York: Wholesale Book Corp., 1972, Book 2, Chapter 1, The Bodily Form, Defects and Accidents: "…Mars exactly rising produces red hair."

3. William Lilly, *The Introduction to Astrology*, 1647, Chapter 7, Of the Planet Mars and His Several Significations: "…their hair red or sandy and may be crisp or curling…."

4. *Brihat Parasara Hora Sastra*, Chapter 3, Planetary Character and Description, p. 322: "Mars has blood red eyes…."

5. William Benham, *The Laws of Scientific Hand Reading*, New York: Hawthorn Books, 1946, p. 284: "The Martian…the hair is short, stiff; sometimes curly and of an auburn or red color."

6. Alan Leo, *The Art of Synthesis*, New York: The Astrologer's Library, 1978 (first pub. 1913), Chapter 8, Mars the Energizer: "…Mars represents a person who is active, strong, energetic, muscular. …hair sometimes red, but not invariably so, occasionally black and often curly or wiry."

7. Annabella Kitson (Ed.), *History and Astrology*, London: Unwin Hyman, 1989, p. 20: "If his indicator is Mars, then he will be red in color with reddish, lanky hair…."

8. H. L. Cornell, M.D., *Encyclopedia of Medical Astrology*, New York: Llewellyn Publications and Samuel Weiser, 1972, p. 280: "…and Mars rising, or a Mars influence or sign in the Asc.; Mars rising trends to give a full face of freckles, and fiery red hair…."

9. Nick Kollerstrom, *The Metal-Planet Relationship*, Bayside, CA: Borderland Sciences Research Foundation, 1993, p. 58.

10. Alison Davidson, *Metal Power*, Bayside, CA: Borderland Sciences Research Foundation, 1991, pp. 27 and 38.

11. Addey's Mars-redhead hypothesis was not identical to Hill and Thompson's. Addey tested for incidence of Mars onjunct all four angles in the birth charts of naturally redheaded people.

12. At the time of publication, an extremely minor correction of two data points was completed for all control groups developed for comparison with redhead groups A, B and C. This minute adjustment will be represented in all upcoming technical reports and does not impact any of the significance claims or graphic examples set forth in this article.

ACKNOWLEDGMENTS

The American Redheads Replication Project Volunteers

Roxanna Muise, Susan Turner, Shelley Brubaker, Rhonda Hoefs, Jennifer Griffith, Susan Scott, Bev Mustin, Dennis Flaherty, Marjorie B. Hunt, Cathy Brenner, Trish Turchiorolo, Rosemary Ardis, Sethyn Bryan, Cathy Bennet, Pam Leneve, Janis Mennona, Sherry Stole, Donna M. Jaeger, Kathryn Alsworth

Provision of Private Data Collections

John Addey, Charles Harvey, Ron Bippus, Beverly Steffert Ph.D., Mike O'Neill, B.Sc.

Data Monitors/Witnesses for the American Redheads Replication Project

Robert Wambach, Ph.D., Susan Payton

Control Groups

Mark Pottenger

REFERENCES

Addey, John
Harmonics, Green Bay, WI: Cambridge Circle, 1977.
Coisnard, Paul
La Hoi d'Heredite Astrale, Paris: Chornac, 1919.
Cornell, Dr. H. L.
Encyclopedia of Medical Astrology, New York: Llewellyn
    Publications and Samuel Weiser, 1972.
Davidson, Alison
Metal Power, Bayside, CA: Borderland Sciences Research
    Foundation, 1991.
Dean, Geoffrey
critique of "The Mars-Redhead Link," *AAJ*, England, 1989.
Douglas, Stephen
The Redhead Dynasty, New Style Communications, 1987.
Gauquelin, Michel
Birth Times, New York: Hill and Wang, 1983.
The Cosmic Clocks, New York: Avon, 1969.
L'Heredite Planetaire, Paris: Denoel, 1966.
critique of "The Mars-Redhead Link," *AAJ*, England, 1989.
"The Nycthemeral Expectancy," *Astro-Psychological Problems*,
    Vol. 3, No.1, 1985.
Hill, Judith A.
"Commentary on the John Addey Redhead Data," NCGR
    Journal Winter 88-89
"The Mars Redhead Link II: Mars distribution Patterns in
    Redhead Populations," *Borderlands, A Quarterly Journal
    of Borderland Research*, Vol, LI, No. 1 (Part I) and No. 2
    (Part II), First and Second Quarter 1995.
"The Regional Factor in Planetary-Seismic Correlation,"
    Borderlands, A Quarterly Journal of Borderland Research,
    Vol, LI, No. 3, Third Quarter 1995.

Hill, Judith A. and Jacalyn Thompson
"The Mars-Redhead Link: A Scientific Test of Astrology," *NCGR Journal*, Winter 88-89. (See sidebar "Medical Anomalies and the Mars-Redhead Link," p. 234.]

Hill, Judith A. and Mark Polit
"Correlation of Earthquakes with Planetary Placement: The Regional Factor," *NCGR Journal*, Vol. 5, No. 1, 1987.

Kollerstrom, Nick
The Metal-Planet Relationship, Bayside, CA: Borderland Sciences Research Foundation, 1991.

Krafft, Karl E.
Traite d'Astrobiologies, Paris: Legrand.

Krucoff, Carol
Psychology Today, 1983

Lakhovsky, Georges
The Secret of Life: Cosmic Rays and Radiations of Living Beings, 1939 (reprinted by Borderland Sciences Research Foundation, Bayside, CA).

Montague, Ashley
Human Heredity, The World Publshing Company, 1983.

O'Neill, Mike
Time-Switching Control Applied to Hill and Thompson's Redhead Data, *Comlation*, June 1991.

Payne, Buryl
"The Comet Jupiter Colision, July 16-23, 1994," *The Mountain Astrologer*, July 1994.

Robinson, Ken
The Canopus Newsletter, 1987.

Steffert, Beverly
"The Mars-Redhead Link Under Attach," *AAJ*, UK.

Thornton, Penny
The Forces of Destiny, London: Weidenfield and Nickleson, 1990.

APPENDIX IV
SECT—DAY OR NIGHT BIRTH

Your birth "Sect" (i.e. day or night birth) acts to magnify certain qualities of the planets. Traditionally, the planets in the east, nearest your Ascending degree of birth, are considered to hold dominance over physical appearance. You might well ask, "How close to my Ascendant does a planet need to be?" The rule is simple: the closer a planet is to your Ascendant degree, the stronger its influence, both physically and temperamentally. The same rule holds true for planets nearest the MC degree. However, this planetary influence is further modified by the sign the planet tenants at birth, and secondarily, the *sect* of your birth. Normally, the sign predominates over sect, although this is not invariably so. Below are described for each Ptolemaic planet the physical and temperamental qualities that birth sect may either enhance or diminish.

You may find this information to be quite useful. For instance, when you see Saturn is exactly conjunct the rising degree of a given individual, you should include sect in your analysis of physical attributes as well as temperament. Should in this case Saturn be in Libra, and the birth was by day, you can expect all that Saturn promises in his masculine condition: exceptional height, extreme leanness, intellect, etc. However, should the birth have occurred at night, and Saturn be in Taurus, you may discover that an entirely different side of Saturn predominates—the earthy! Don't be too surprised should a square, dense, and rather clunky individual in gardener's clothes walks through your door because here we have the feminine face of Saturn—not the wise man, but instead, the patient, responsible builder.

HOW TO KNOW YOUR SECT

If you were born when the Sun was *above* the horizon (between the Ascendant and Descendant, going clockwise from Ascendant), then you are born in the *Day* Sect. If your Birth Sun is *under* the horizon (beneath the Ascendant and Descendant degrees, anti-clockwise from Ascendant), then you were born in the *Night* Sect.

SUN

Day Sect: Enhances and magnifies all Solar properties. This is especially so should the Sun be in a Fire sign.

Night sect: Reduces Solar qualities. This is especially so should the Sun be in an Air, Earth or Water sign.

MOON

Day Sect: Reduces all lunar qualities. This is especially so should the Moon be in a Fire or Air sign (Fire most).

Night sect: Enhances and magnifies all lunar qualities. This is especially so should the Moon be in an Earth or Water sign (strongest in Cancer, Pisces and Taurus).

VENUS

Day Sect: Resembles Libra. The refined, slender and willowy side of Venus is enhanced. Doubly so if Venus is in an Air or Fire sign (most for Air). Magnifies the Venusian tendency toward sociability, culture, diplomacy, and grace.

Night sect: Resembles Taurus. The softer, fuller featured side of Venus is enhanced. Doubly so if Venus is in an Earth or Water sign. Magnifies the Venusian tendency toward pleasure, self-indulgence, sensuality, art, and beauty.

MERCURY

Day Sect: Resembles Gemini. The taller, fluent, expressive, and playful side of Mercury is enhanced. Doubly so if Mercury is in an Air sign. Magnifies Mercury's tendency toward versatility, mobility, innovative intellect, communication, instability, change, and wit.

Night sect: The petite, well-knit, skillful, and exacting side of Mercury is enhanced. Doubly so if Mercury is in an Earth sign. Magnifies Mercury's tendency toward specialization precision, practical intellect, observation of facts, and astuteness.

MARS

Day Sect: Resembles Aries. The hot, ruddy, lean, muscular and lighter side of Mars is enhanced. Doubly so if Mars is in Fire or Air signs (strongest in Fire). Magnifies Mars' tendency toward excitability, irritability, courage, initiative, and temper.

Night sect: Resembles Scorpio. The dark, intense, thicker side of Mars is enhanced. Highly sexed and hirsute. Stronger for Mars in an Earth or Water sign. Magnifies Mars' tendency toward strategy, stamina, control, strength, endurance, brutality, and concealment.

SATURN

Day Sect: Resembles Libra and Aquarius. The tall, bony side of Saturn is enhanced. Doubly so if Saturn is in a Fire or Air sign. Magnifies Saturn's tendency toward wisdom, intellect, authority, leadership and solitude.

Night Sect: Resembles Earth signs. The strong, dense, and shorter side of Saturn is enhanced. Big bones, tough constitution with exceptional endurance. Doubly so if Saturn is in a Water or Earth sign. Magnifies Saturn's tendency toward responsibility, duty and building.

JUPITER

Day Sect: Resembles Sagittarius. Expands upward. The taller, athletic side of Jupiter is enhanced. Doubly so if Jupiter is in a Fire or Air sign (Fire is strongest). Magnifies Jupiter's tendency toward extravagance, egocentricity, leadership and command.

Night sect: Resembles Pisces. Expands outward. The rounder, fatter side of Jupiter is enhanced. Stronger for Jupiter in Water or Earth signs (especially strong in Cancer and Pisces). Magnifies Jupiter's tendency toward benevolence, compassion and indulgence.

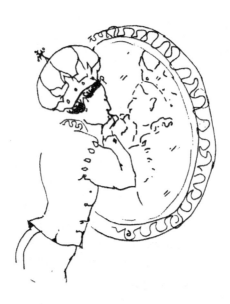

APPENDIX V
MEDICAL ELEMENTS

The four elements of antiquity can be seen as a structural thread running through theoretical reams as diverse as physiognomy and Jungian psychology. However, it is in western medical astrology that the four elements stand alone in purest form, unencumbered by abstractions and theories imposed by the less physically oriented sciences. To acquaint the reader with these four elements and their use in early western medicine is the purpose of this work. First, we must introduce a few basics.

The four elements represent four planes of matter (and much more as will be described later). Classical astrology assigns each of the twelve zodiacal signs to one of the four elements: Fire, Earth, Air or Water. The Fire, Air, Water and Earth signs form our first and simplest description of zodiacal types useful to the early physicians. At birth, the weight of planetary distribution within each of the elements paints an astrophysical portrait of the elemental balance within both psyche and body. An observation of the planetary birth map allows us to discover the weakest elements in our physical and psychological makeup and also the most dominant. Frequently, we emotionally feel and physically see the dominant element of a friend before perhaps guessing their more particular zodiac sign type.

However, what exactly are these four elements? In fact, the four elements can be viewed esoterically, spiritually, psychologically, and physically. Fire, Earth, Air and Water describe four levels of concretization of matter, four states of awareness, four temperaments and four types of matter within the chemical-molecular universe. This explains why the astrologers, Jungian psychologists and medieval physicians have each defined the four elements variously and utilized their knowledge of them for quite separate purposes.

THE ELEMENTS AS LEVELS OF THE CONCRETIZATION OF MATTER

In the most arcane sense, the elements refer to four levels of increasing concretization of matter: photon, particle, atom and molecule. One can think of this concretization as the journey of light (the photon, as the Fire element) from complete freedom (Fire) into gradually denser and more predictable forms, represented first by Air and then Water. Finally finding itself "trapped" in the densest plane of the molecule, symbolized as the stodgy, reliable Earth element. As the photon journeys from creation towards material expression (particle, atom, molecule), it gathers weight experience and form while sacrificing the playfulness and freedom of the photon and particle.

THE FOUR ELEMENTS AND THE FOUR WORLDS

The four levels of concretization of matter directly correspond to the four planes or worlds of the Cabalists. Their highest or Spiritual World, Atziluth is the world of emanations and archetypes. Atziluth corresponds best with the photon and with the Fire element. The second plane, Briah, constitutes the world of thought and creation. Briah belongs to the world of particles and to the thinking element Air. Similarly, the malleable Astral World, known to Cabalists as Yetzirah, the world of formations, corresponds to the atom and the receptive, impressionable, and feeling oriented Water element. Last, the Physical Plane (or Chemical-Molecular Plane) is the realm of the molecule and is represented by the densest element, Earth. Cabalists know this fourth world as Assiah, the world of action and the world of matter. As denizens of Assiah, we find ourselves at present confined largely to the laws of the material plane.

THE FOUR ELEMENTS AS FOUR TYPES OF CONSCIOUSNESS

The four elements are also commonly described as four types of consciousness. Jung, who studied astrology and read horoscopes, adopted these traditional four awarenesses as his famous four psychological types. However, these four types are neither Jung's invention nor anything new to astrologers who have used them for millennia.

Fire symbolizes pure being, the sense of "I," and the life force. It is direct experience. Jung made this his famous "intuitive" type. Air represents the intellect. This is the world of thought, language and abstraction. Its mode of consciousness is detached observation. Jung renamed Air his "thinking" type. Our receptive feeling function is Water. Emotions and instincts arise from this level. Water is responsive and a subjective experience. A person with this type of awareness Jung termed a "feeling" type. Earth represents sensation, and the body. This is the densest of the four levels and corresponds to body consciousness, materiality, survival, and the structuring, body building function. Jung christened Earth as his "sensate" type.

THE FOUR TEMPERAMENTS

Medieval physicians classified four "humors" of the body, and associated these with four physiognomical and temperamental types termed Choleric (Fire), Sanguine (Air), Phlegmatic (Water), and Melancholic (Earth). We do not have the space here to commence a detailed discussion of the four humors and corresponding temperaments. It is enough to say that the four temperaments, though physiognomical, also roughly correspond to Jung's four astrologically based psychological types although in some writings the Melancholic or Earth type is viewed as entirely negative, which is inaccurate.

In this system, a balance of the four humors produced a balanced temperament and a state of good health. Disease was a manifestation of an imbalance of these humors. A similar idea continues today in modern Ayurvedic practice, with one exception. The four humors of the body have been grouped into just three doshas, or elemental forces. Air becomes Vata, Fire is Pitta, and Water and Earth combine in a single "heavy" humor known as Kapha. the description of the Kapha type appears to combine the qualities of the traditional western Phlegmatic and Melancholic psychological temperaments. Fruits, vegetables, medicines and activities are also classed under each dosha. Healing is assisted by subscribing to a regimen that balances these doshas. If you are too hot, then you must cool off. If you are too damp, then you must dry out, and so forth.

THE FOUR ELEMENTS AS FOUR TYPES OF MATTER

This is very simple. The element Fire manifests as fire. The element Air as air. Water is water, and Earth is earth. However, their correspondences to the physical body are a bit more complex.

Fire is the Chinese "Chi" or life force, also the energy and the digestive force. Fire releases energy. Therefore, the metabolic and fuel burning activities of the body take place through activation of the Fire element. The action of Fire is hot, light, and dry.

Air governs the little known electrical forces and connections within the body, neurotransmission, motion, oxygen-ation of the blood, breath, language, and motion. Its action is cold, light and moist (some texts say alternatively cold, light, and dry).

Water rules the waters of the body. This includes phlegm, lymph, semen and all other bodily secretions and fluids. The moist and protective mucous membranes of the body are a function of the Water element. Also, our memory function is related to Water because Water is the most impressionable of elements. The action of Water upon the body is cold, heavy and wet.

Earth governs the minerals within the body, the bones and the building of a bodily structure. Earth also holds in energy and has much to do with stamina, food storage, body building and longevity. Earth is warm, heavy and dry (the Earth sign Taurus may be an exception, producing more a warm and moist condition). Natives in Taurus, the preeminent Earth sign, are noted for being human greenhouses, always maintaining a warm body temperature.

THE RATE OF MATTER IN MOTION: THE THREE MODES

In the simplest context, the four elements are four states of matter: light, liquid, gas and mineral. As said earlier, each of the twelve signs are assigned to one of the four elements. This classification is accomplished in the folowing manner:

Fire — Aries, Leo, Sagittarius
Air — Gemini, Libra, Aquarius
Water — Cancer, Scorpio, Pisces
Earth — Taurus, Virgo, Capricorn

However there is a further sign classification of great import. Because matter moves, we must sub designate each element according to the rate of matter in motion. This produces the three Modes or Quadruplicities of classical western astrology. It is these modes that describe the rate of matter in motion. These three rates are known as the Cardinal, Mutable and Fixed modes. For instance, Fire igniting is Cardinal Fire. The concentrated Fire of an oven is Fixed Fire in action. A wildfire would be, of course, Mutable Fire, or moving fire. Cardinal energy always initiates each season. Fixed energy always occurs in mid-season, such as midsummer when the energy of Fixed Fire (heat, dryness) is most concentrated. Mutable energy is transitional and dispersive, always occurring at the end of a season as it gradually changes into the following quarter.

The Cardinal signs of astrology are those signs that mark the two solstice and the two equinox points: Aries, Cancer, Libra and Capricorn. They are active and initiating in nature (one may argue the reverse in the case of indecisive Libra if one fails to reason that Libra initiates the Air qualities of abstract contemplativeness and detached observation). The Fixed signs are the stubborn four: Taurus, Leo, Scorpio and Aquarius. Mutable signs are noted for their versatile, flexible and sometimes unstable natures: Gemini, Virgo, Sagittarius and Pisces.

IMBALANCES OF THE FOUR ELEMENTS AND HEALTH

Imbalance of the four elements occurs in one of two ways: deficiency or excess. Your planetary birth chart is the tool used by astrologers to divine the quality and amount of each element in the birth chart. Until the mid-seventeenth century, physicians were required to have passed their exams in astrology. Each physician was expected to be fluent in the diagnosis of planetary charts from the medical perspective. The complex nature of this astro-medical analysis is beyond the scope of this article. Instead, I would like to present a listing of common complaints associated with both the excesses and deficiencies of each element. A few interesting cases from my own files will round out the discussion.

FIRE EXCESS

Dehydration, hyperactivity, hyperthyroid, baldness, emaciation, great hunger, brainstorms, aneurysm, heart attack, high blood pressure, stroke, overheating, sunstroke, insomnia, liver disturbances, egomania, compulsive behaviors, itch, inflammation, alcoholism, boils, acne eruptions, arterial and blood vessel complaints, hyperstress.

Antidote: The Water Element.
Treatment: Hydration with cool liquids, cool baths, cool moist

herbs and foods, sweet and moist foods, fruits, green color, calm music, avoid hot, spicy and oily foods, avoid red colors, stay away from hot sun, avoid overheating, apply liver tonics and purification, strengthen arteries, avoid temper and excessive excitement.

FIRE DEFICIENT
Weak, listless, hypoenergetic, overweight, low blood pressure, depression poor eyesight, poor self-esteem, fatigued, poor digestive fire, weak heart.

Balance: Apply Fire.
Treatments: Exercise, heart and blood tonics, red stones and colors, dance and play therapy, brass instruments and rousing music, iron, spices, improve circulation, develop muscles of upper body, sing, paint.

FIRE FIELD NOTES
Here is an interesting case of Fire excess extracted from my files. A friend of mine gave birth to a redheaded baby boy. Soon after birth he became badly dehydrated, fitful and would rage all night. He had great difficulty sleeping. His birth chart showed not only an excess of astrological hot and dry Fire signs but none of the balancing moist Water signs, plus a very prominent Mars near the Ascendant at birth—Mars, of course, is a hot and dry planet. Upon hearing this, the mother had the invention and insight to do something to bring the Water element into the baby's energy field. She began soaking him in a comfortable bath just before bed! Baby loved his baths and afterward slept sweetly, his crying problem greatly diminished from the onset of the Water experiments.

Fire deficiency frequently manifests as a lack of confidence and a weak ego. The individual lacks playfulness, warmth, creativity and pizzazz. They may also lack the ability to initiate activities. One case of deficient Fire combined with excess Earth is most interesting. This man suffered from an absolutely compulsive need to seek stimulating entertainment and social events. He craved stimulation (Fire) from outside because he could not find it within. However, despite his constant socializing, he was personally so introverted and reserved that he could hardly carry on a conversation and had the greatest difficulty expressing himself in any way, or displaying affection. Outwardly, he appeared cold, rather lifeless and unresponsive. Inwardly he possessed much stamina (Earth), and was a capable long distance runner.

AIR EXCESS
Scattered, nervous, excess talking, mentally unbalanced or fatigued, mental flights, hyperactive, restless, cold, anemia arthritic, hypersensitive, emaciated, unstable, thin and balding hair, lacks personality force, weakness, self-destructive through irregular living, indecisive, scattered.

Antidote: Earth.

Treatment: Good nutrition, mineral baths and tonics, warmth, nature, massage, practicality, gain weight, business training, weight lifting, warm, solid, and well prepared meals every day, warm grains, root foods, calming music, quiet time, sleep, sedatives, nervines and mental rest, yellow and blue colors.

AIR DEFICIENT
Asthma, sub-oxygenation of cells, lung weakness, poor judgment, lack of humor, listless, overly intense (Air lightens), slow in thought or movement, poor circulation, weak heart action, low blood pressure.

Balance: Apply Air.

Breathing exercises, improve bodily oxygenation and circulation, humor therapy, views, mental development exercises, fresh air, juggling, coordination exercises, speech therapy, flexibility exercises, yoga, strengthen the lungs and arms.

AIR FIELD NOTES
Over the years a number of clients have arrived with deficient

Air element. I always then ask the question: "Do you have asthma, shortness of breath or bronchitis?" Their reply is typically affirmative. It is evident that Air deficient people do indeed lack oxygen! Lack of air may also manifest on the mental plane as lack of levity, comparative reasoning or objectivity.

A recent case was that of a young woman with many talents. However, she could not acquire appropriate schooling for lack of ability with tests and memorization of facts. She simply could not learn through the standard western educational method. She took readily to my suggestion that she might do better in an experimental type of educational setting.

Air excess produces the scattered, unsettled and over talkative individual. This type spurns routine and does not take good care of themselves. Smoking cigarettes, irregular sleeping, sexual and eating habits, plus frequent job changes all give rise to fatigued nerves and an unsettled mental condition. Although seemingly able to burn the candles at both ends without mishap, the Air type will burn themselves out early and not infrequently expires before their time. Tuberculosis, nervous breakdown, mental disturbances and malnutrition are complaints common to excess Air, especially when coupled with a deficient Earth element. In cases of excess Air, the Ayruvedic physician insists on a stable routine combined with warm grains, oils and vegetables. Cold foods and beverages are forbidden as are excesses of all kinds.

WATER EXCESS
Water retention, bloat, nausea, fermentations, yeast, sluggishness, low energy, oversleeping, drowsy, over-sexed, indulgent, dependent and addictive behaviors, obese, paranoid, tender swellings, pain sensitive, overly emotional and childish, lazy, depressed, chills, weak eyesight, poor structure and posture, weak teeth and bones, shuns daylight, avoids reality, introversion, noise sensitivity, soft growths and tumors, breast lumps, prostrate swellings, excess mucous and other bodily fluids.

Antidote: Fire.

Treatment: Purgatives, sweats, promote urination, hot spices, exercise, dry heat, heat lamps, cognitive therapy, sunlight, laughter, warm colors, stimulation, affection. Avoid cold wet and sweet foods (ice cream and watermelon are the worst for this type), improve heart action and circulation. The Water type responds excellently to kindness.

WATER DEFICIENT

Insomnia, restless and overactive, dehydrated, dry, inability to relax, constipated, infertile, low libido or sex satisfaction, fears or alternatively craves intimacy, low appetites, insensitive, memory dysfunction, paranoia, complaints of dryness, swallowing, etc.

Balance: Apply Water.

Treatment: Swim and bathe, humidifiers, drink liquids, exposure to moonlight, pearls, silver, dolphins, puddings and custards, romantic music, sleep, sedatives, psychotherapy, psyllium seed, slippery elm bark, chanting, herbal laxatives, comfrey root and similar demulcents to moisten the mucous membranes, aphrodisiacs, nurturing (receiving or giving), support groups, lakes, rivers, and oceans, boating, fishing, meditating, devotional, and charitable work.

WATER FIELD NOTES

In my work a number of interesting cases have appeared of persons born with a great excess in the Water signs In most of these cases, should a lack of the drying Fire element also fail to be present, you will find the dropsical and water laden body. Two cases demonstrate Water excess most effectively. One case was of a girl who spent most of her life in a semi-coma following a botched operation for a brain tumor. This unfortunately individual was very sensitive, sweet and passive, and eventually passed on at a young age. A similar case of being "under water" is that of Helen Keller, born deaf, dumb and blind. She was also born with a considerable excess of planets in the astrological Water signs. However, despite her unusual condition, this individual achieved much and the malady appeared to be restricted to the physical condition.

Three cases of Water deficiency recently observed produced individuals who suffered from a lack of inner peace. Water is the element of peace, and so this makes good sense. Both individuals were restless, suffered insomnia and found it impossible to relax or to enjoy intimacy. One friend, who completely lacked the Water element and yet possessed much Fire, compulsively spent her money and traveled. This strange behavior was symptomatic of excessive Fire, and Air energy. (Fire burns fuel rapidly and blasts outward, and Air assists in the process of combustion). She was seized with intense ambitions that would abruptly change with the wind. Her dry and hard body completely lacked the subcutaneous fat typical of the feminine sex. In this case, a medieval physician might attempt to introduce the Water and possibly Earth elements into the body while simultaneously cooling down the Fire element and balancing the Air element.

EARTH EXCESS
Mental dullness, lack of mental creativity, either boring or suffers a chronic sense of boredom, withholding, laconic, overeats and overworks, the body is either sluggish and very large and heavy or very bony and emaciated—curious! (The weight extreme observed will depend on a number of other factors.) Suffers dryness, constipation, dandruff, skin problems, eczema, brittle nails and cuticles (dry), mucous membranes also dry, brittle teeth, hearing problems. Unresponsive and insensitive. Generally strong and healthy on a daily level, although highly prone to chronic conditions and cancer due to toxic buildups, constipation, arthritis and rheumatism, bone spurs, hard growths, cancer. Great longevity.

Antidote: Air, then Water.

Treatment: Purgatives, colonic therapy, fasting, saunas, vegetarianism, emotional and affectional development, light eating of light foods, flexibility exercises, dexterity exercises, oil rubs and compresses, conversation, variety, travel, mental stimulation (improve mental speed verbal and comparative faculties), humor, neurological stimulation, development of social fluidity, demulcent herbs to moisten the mucous membranes, avoidance of rich, toxic, or dry foods such as meat, milk products and pastries, breathing exercises, views and flying, reading and writing, hatha yoga.

EARTH DEFICIENT

Difficulty in gaining or holding weight or money, low stamina, weak bones and teeth, poor physical strength and endurance, weak posture and bodily structure, poor appetite, nervous, impractical, unstable, cold, insufficient immunity, hypothermia, cold body, malnutrition, mineral deficiency, ungrounded.

Balance: Apply Earth.

Treatment: Minerals, mud and mineral baths, nature, sitting on the earth, hatha yoga, stable routine, weight lifting, aikido, Tai Chi and other exercises that teach one to hold in energy, warmth, massage and touch, steady jobs, herbal therapies, calcium, good food, gardening, building, pottery, sculpture, business training and money management, improve attention to clothing and appearance.

EARTH FIELD NOTES

As in other elements, an excess or deficiency of Earth becomes more apparent with the simultaneous appearance of an opposite condition (excess/deficiency) for another element. Two individuals that spring to mind are by temperament matter-of-fact, never dramatic and lack complexity; both possess excess Earth and deficient Fire. They are slow moving, yet thorough and dedicated in all endeavors undertaken. Their bodies are dense and sluggish, as is their speech. One of the two suffered a hearing complaint typical of Earth signs. Their bones, hands and feet were large and clumsy. Physically, they were always very warm. Remember, Earth is a greenhouse—it holds in heat; whereas Fire lets it out! Earth is a very tough, dense element and so are excessively earthy people. It is not therefore unremarkable that a number of the great heavyweight boxers (including Rocky Marciano, Foreman, Frasier, and Muhammad Ali) were born in Earth signs. It would be interesting to make a statistical study of Earth signs in the birth charts of boxers. Curiously, other Earth type people I've observed are of the bony "ectomorphic" category. This is due to the rulership of Saturn over the Earth sign Capricorn. This Saturnian type Earth element person may be bony but they are dependably tough and strong, with excellent stamina. Both Earth types make excellent gardeners.

A case of Earth deficiency with strong Air came with a man who was finding it impossible to find a home. And although he made good money, stability evaded him. He did not understand money or the material universe very well and was ever in danger of being conned by the more worldly wise. Mentally he was agitated and fearful of dealing with life's realities. Remember, Earth signs deal with the Earth plane. Sometimes he would forget to eat, and possessed no materialistic desire to own anything. His body was exceptionally fragile, and he suffered a lifelong trouble with stamina (Earth element), rendering him incapable of prolonged physical labor. He could do anything a little while, but just could not physically keep up on the long hike. It was important to him to spend time in nature (Earth) every day. Nature calmed his sensitive nerves and provided the quiet he longed for more than anything else.

This man tended to insufficient digestion of nutrients leading to mineral deficiencies and benefited from minerals taken through sea water extracts. Earthy staples such as grains and potatoes were favorite foods although he could not eat too much at one sitting without difficulty. It was important for him to lift weights only to maintain his delicate frame in good health. Curiously, he was greatly attracted to granite and other heavy rocks and loved to sit on boulders overlooking natural scenes. As a rule, he suffered greatly from cold and seemed unable to produce or contain his own heat. Hypothermia was ever a danger. The only way he could warm up was through application of hot baths and a glass of hot tea before bed. In all probability, a medieval physician would have him apply hot earth, mud or mineral compresses instead, to replenish the missing Earth element.

THE ELEMENTS IN COMBINATION

The above descriptions are simple compared to the actual practice of medical astrology. The four elements are never observed in a vacuum. Any elemental excess present in the planetary birth chart automatically signals the reader that some other element must be deficient. This fact gives rise to several classifications of deficient/excess element pairs, too numerous to discuss in this present article. Additionally, the entire birth chart is taken under consideration. The planets in particular are observed for sign placement, and also according to their temperature, hearkening back to and supportive of the four elements. For instance, Mars is a hot and dry planet and Saturn is cold and dry. However, should you be born at night with Mars appearing above the horizon and in a cooling Water or Earth sign, then the normally destructive nature of Mars is toned down through this cooler, moister situation. Similarly, Saturn benefits by placement in a warming day birth, especially when placed above the horizon in a warm masculine sign.

A CASE OF ELEMENTS ACTING TOGETHER
FIELD NOTES:

An extremely interesting case recently came to my attention. This is the case of a young man with an excess of both Earth and Fire, acting in combination with a condition which can only be described as disturbed Water. The disturbed Water element was brought about in the following manner: the moist Moon was in the hot and dry Fire element and strongly afflicted by Mars, a hot, drying planet. To compound matters, Mars was the only planet located in the Water element. This created an extremely dry and agitated condition within the body.

Repeatedly, the boy was hospitalized for severe dehydration. He could not drink or eat and his stomach rejected not only foods but liquids. Severe constipation, difficulty swallowing, and partial deafness accompanied the foregoing symptoms. Remember, Water rules the mucous membranes; in this boy's case Water is not only weak, but suffers from an intrusion of the Fire element, further damaging Water's soothing and moisturizing properties. The excess of Earth in the birth chart created a dry, dull, and listless appearance. The Air element was also weak, exacerbating the combination of excess Earth and Fire with disturbed Water. As a rarefied element, Air acts to assist the burning rate of Fire, which smolders intensely without enough Air. Also, a satisfactory Air element would prevent the Earth element from becoming too heavy and absorbing. Could the ancient elemental medicine bring relief for this unfortunate case?

CONCLUSION

The medical use of the four elements has never died, continuing to the present time in dual form. In the East, the respected practice of Ayurvedic medicine relies heavily upon the consideration of the elements (*doshas*) for diagnosis and treatment. In Europe, the entirety of medical astrology inclusive of the four medical elements was forced underground at the close of the seventeenth century. However, despite the prevailing opposition against the practice of Western astro-medicine, its use and knowledge have never died and its principles continue to be utilized by a small number of licensed Western physicians.

Davidson's excellent *Medical Lectures* (out of print) and Dr. Cornell's *Encyclopedia of Medical Astrology* are but a few cases in point. One cannot peruse the contents of these writings without being suitably impressed with the complexity and sophistication of twentieth century medical astrology. Other interesting examples might be Dr. Margaret Millard's *Case Notes of a Medical Astrologer* and Carl Jansky's *Modern Medical Astrology*.

Those that practice medical astrology are certain of its efficacy. Personally, I've witnessed cases where the cause of a hidden health complaint eludes the doctors while the answer sits crystal clear in the horoscope waiting to be seen by all. Eventually, and after many tests, if not enormous cost to the hapless patient, the doctors finally discover the source of the mystery problem to be identical with the astrologer's diagnosis. Could it be that the ancient physicians were on to something after all?

BIBLIOGRAPHY

BOOKS

Ptolemy's Tetrabiblios, Claudius Ptolemy, 140 A.D., reprinted, The Aries Press, Chicago, IL, 1936.

The Love and Lure of Outer Space, Ernst and Johanna Lehren, Tudor Publishing Company, NY, 1964.

The Key to Astrology, Raphael, Health Research, Mokelumne Hill, CA.

Brihat Parasara Hora Sastra, Maharshi Parasara, Vols. I & II: Ranjan Publishers, New Delhi, India, 1992.

From the River of Heaven, David Frawley, Passage Press, Salt Lake City, UT, 1990.

Birth Times, Michel Gauquelin, Hill and Wang, New York, NY 1983.

Studies in Character Analysis, Manly P. Hall, The Philosophical Research Society, Inc., Los Angeles, CA, 1958.

Astrological Types, Howard M. Duff, Howard M. Duff, 1948

The Face Finder, M. M. Gerasimov, Hutchison and Co., Ltd., Great Britain, 1971.

The Moon's Nodes, George White, American Federation of Astrologers, 1927.

Know Your Ascendant for Accurate Horoscope Making, Dr. Chancey D. King, American Federation of Astrologers, Tempe, AZ, 1966.

Man and the Zodiac, David Anrias, E.P. Dutton and Company, New York, 1938.

Reading Faces, Leopold Bellak, M.D. & Samm Sinclair Baker, Bantam Books, New York, NY, 1983

Analyzing Character, Katherine M. H. Blackford, M.D. and Arthur Newcomb, The Review of Reviews Company, 1916.

Character Analysis, Jean Morris Ellis, (Second Edition) Jean Morris Ellis, Los Angeles, CA., 1929.

The A to Z Horoscope Maker and Delineator, Llewellyn George, Llewellyn Publication, St. Paul, MN, 1970.

About Faces, Terry Landau, Anchor Books, New York, NY, 1989.

An Introduction to Astrology, William Lilly, Newcastle Publishing, CA, 1972 (1647).

Face Reading, Timothy T. Mar, Signet, New York, NY, 1975.

Eye Language, E. Marshall, New Trend Publishers, Toronto, Ontario, 1983.

The Manual of Astrology, Sepharial, Wholesale Books, NYC, 1972.

Characterology, Carl E. Wagner, Jr., Samuel Weiser, York Beach, ME, 1986.

The Art of Synthesis, Alan Leo, England, 1926.

Encyclopedia of Medical Astrology, H. L. Cornell, M.D., Llewellyn Publications and Samuel Weiser, Inc., NYC, 1972.

Astrological Physiognomy, G. Barrett, Aries Press, Chicago, IL, 1941.

The Law of Scientific Handwriting, by William G. Benham, Hawthorn Books Inc., 1946.

JOURNAL ARTICLES

The Mars-Redhead Link; Judith A. Hill & Jacalyn Thompson, NCGR Journal, Winter 1988. First published by Above and Below, Toronto, Cananda, Summer, 1988.

Redheads and the Gauquelin Effect, J. Lee Lehman, Ph.D., NCGR Journal, Winter '88.

Commentary on the John Addey Redhead Data, NCGR Journal, Judith A. Hill, 1988.

Time Switching Control Applied to Hill & Thompson's Redhead Data, Mike O'Neill, Correlations, December 1990, England.

Astrology and Genetics - Red Hair, The Astrological Journal, (UK) Vol. 10, No. 3, pp 5-18 (1968).

Congenital Malformation and Season of Birth, J. C. Bailser and J. Gurian, Eugenics Quarterly, Vol. 12, pp 146-153 (1966).

BOOKS BY AUTHOR

The Astrological Body Types, revised & expanded, Stellium Press, 1997, available through Book People, A. F. A. Inc. Russian and Lettish language editions available through Astroinformservis, Latvia.

The Part of Fortune in Astrology, Stellium Press, 1998, revised, 2010.

Vocational Astrology: A Complete Handbook of Western Astrological Career Selection and Guidance Techniques, A. F. A. Inc., 1999.

The Mars-Redhead Files, Stellium Press, 2000 (compendium of published astro-genetic research by Hill and Hill-Thompson).

Astroseismology: Earthquakes and Astrology, Stellium Press, 2000 compendium of published research by Hill and Hill-Polit).

Medical Astrology: A Guide to Planetary Pathology, Stellium Press, 2005.

Mrs. Winkler's Cure, Stellium Press, 2010 (original fairy tales published under pen name Julia Holly).

The Lunar Nodes: Your Key to Excellent Chart Interpretation, Stellium Press, 2010.

A Wonderbook of True Astrological Case Files (co-authored with Andrea L. Gehrz), Moira Press, 2012.

Eclipses and You, Stellium Press, 2013

JOURNAL ARTICLES

"Correlation of Earthquakes with Planetary Placement: The Regional Factor," Judith A. Hill and Mark Polit, *NCGR Journal,* 5 (1), 1987.

"The Mars–Redhead Link," Judith A. Hill & Jacalyn Thompson, *NCGR Journal,* Winter 88-89 (first published by *Above & Below* (Canada); *Linguace Astrale* (Italy); *AA Journal* (Great Britain); *FAA Journal* (Australia).

"The Mars Redhead Link II: Mars Distribution Patterns in Redhead Populations", *Borderlands Research Sciences Foundation Journal,* Vol. L1, No 1 (Part 1) and Vol. L1, No 2 (Part 2).

"Commentary on the John Addey Redhead Data," *NCGR Journal,* Winter 88-89.

"Redheads and Mars," *The Mountain Astrologer*, May, 1996.

"The Regional Factor in Planetary-Seismic Correlation," *Borderlands Research Sciences Foundation Journal*, Vol. L1, Number 3, 1995 (reprint courtesy of *American Astrology*).

"American Redhead's Project Replication," *Correlation*, Volume 13, No 2, Winter 94-95.

"Octaves of Time," *Borderlands Research Journal*, Vol. L1, Number 4, Fourth Quarter, 1995

"Gemstones, Antidotes for Planetary Weaknesses," *ISIS Journal*, 1994.

"Medical Astrology," *Borderlands Research Journal*, Vol. L11, Number 1, First Quarter, 1996.

"Astrological Heredity," *Borderlands Research Journal*, 1996.

"The Electional and Horary Branches," *Sufism, IAS*, Vol. 1, No 2.

"Astrology: A Philosophy of Time & Space," *Sufism, IAS*, Vol. 1, No 1.

"Natal Astrology," *Sufism, IAS*, Vol. 1, No 3.

"An Overview of Medical Astrology," *Sufism, IAS*, Vol. 1, No 4.

"Predictive Astrology in Theory & Practice," *Sufism, IAS*, Vol. 11, No 1.

"Esoteric Astrology," *Sufism, IAS*, Vol. 11, No 2, 3.

"Mundane Astrology," *SSufism, IAS*, Vol. 11, No 4.

"Vocational Astrology," *Sufism, IAS*, Parts 1 and 2, Vol. 111, No 1, 2.

"Astro-Psychology," *Sufism, IAS*, Vol. 111, No 3, 4.

"The Planetary Time Clocks," *Sufism, IAS*, Vol. 4, No 1, 2, 3, 4.

"Astrophysiognomy," *Sufism, IAS*, Vol. 4, No 1, 2.

"Spiritual Signposts in the Birth Map," *Sufism, IAS*, Vol. V, No 2, 3.

"The Philosophical Questions Most Frequently Asked of the Astrologer," *Sufism, IAS*, Vol. 5, No 4, Vol. 6, No 1, 2.

"Music and the Ear of the Beholder," *Sufism, IAS*, 1999.

"The Astrology of Diabetes," Dell Horoscope, October, 2003.

"A Life Time in Astrology," Interview with the author, by Tony Howard, *The Mountain Astrologer*, Dec., 2011.

CPSIA information can be obtained at www.ICGtesting.com
Printed in the USA
BVOW06s1649130715

408332BV00007B/172/P